Lesson Essentials, Grades 3-8

Denice Luczak

Thank you for participating in the UCSD STEM Project.

You are a leader of successful STEM education.
June 30, 2013

STEM

Lesson Essentials, Grades 3-8

Integrating Science, Technology, Engineering, and Mathematics

Jo Anne Vasquez
Cary Sneider
and Michael Comer

Foreword by Rodger Bybee

HEINEMANN
Portsmouth, NH

Heinemann
361 Hanover Street
Portsmouth, NH 03801–3912
www.heinemann.com

Offices and agents throughout the world

The authors and publisher wish to thank those who have generously given permission to reprint borrowed material:

Excerpts from *Common Core State Standards* © Copyright 2010. National Governors Association Center for Best Practices and Council of Chief State School Officers. All rights reserved.

Excerpts from *A Framework for K–12 Science Education: Practices, Crosscutting Concepts, and Core Ideas* by the National Academy of Sciences (2012). Reprinted by permission of The National Academies Press, Washington, DC.

Figures 9.1a, 9.1b, 9.4a, and 9.4b: "East Cootie Bug and West Cootie Bug" drawings by Michael Biewener. Reprinted by permission of the illustrator.

"Where Is Away?" adapted from *The Waste Hierarchy: Where Is "Away"?* by the Lawrence Hall of Science, University of California, Berkeley's Science Education for Public Understanding Program (SEPUP). Copyright © 1993, 2003 by the Regents of the University of California. Reprinted by permission of SEPUP, Lawrence Hall of Science, University of California, Berkeley.

"Seven Practices for Effective Learning" by Jay McTighe and Ken O'Connor from *Educational Leadership*, vol. 63, no. 3, pp. 7–17 (November 2005). Copyright © 2010 by ASCD. Adapted and used with permission. Learn more about ASCD at www.ascd.org.

Cataloging-in-Publication Data is on file with the Library of Congress.

ISBN: 978-0-325-04358-6

Editor: Katherine Bryant
Production editor: Sonja S. Chapman
Typesetter: Cape Cod Compositors, Inc.
Cover and interior designs: Bernadette Skok
Manufacturing: Steve Bernier

Printed in the United States of America on acid-free paper

16   15   14   13   VP   2   3   4   5

CONTENTS

ACKNOWLEDGMENTS

We sincerely appreciate the extraordinary efforts of the following individuals whose work is prominently featured in *STEM Lesson Essentials*: Jake Prokop, whose description in Chapter 15 of an innovative and engaging middle school STEM unit demonstrates the benefits of collaboration; Mariel Milano, who worked with teachers and administrators throughout her school district to break down the silos between the disciplines and wrote about it in Chapter 16; and Stacey Greene, whose inspirational STEM unit is featured in Chapters 1 and 4.

Thanks also to our Editor at Heinemann, Katherine Bryant, who encouraged us to begin this project and provided guidance along the way, as well as others at our publisher, especially Sonja Chapman, Production Editor, Hilary Zusman, Editorial Coordinator, Bernadette Skok, who designed the cover, and Michael Biewener, who drew the images of "Cooties" in Chapter 9.

We also thank the following individuals for giving us permission to include their programs in this book: Barbara Nagle, Director of SEPUP at the Lawrence Hall of Science, and Nadja Anderson, BIOTECH Project Director at the University of Arizona.

Finally, we thank the many individuals whose projects and ideas are cited and referenced throughout the book, and the many individuals who have personally shared their knowledge and love of teaching. And perhaps most important, we are deeply grateful to our students—many of whom are now adults—whose enthusiastic responses to our classes have shaped our own ideas about teaching and learning across the decades.

FOREWORD

After reviewing STEM Lesson Essentials, Grades 3–8, I write this foreword with great optimism about STEM education and its influence in education. The authors have done a great service by completing this informative and practical book. Let me clarify this positive evaluation.

For several years now, I have paid attention to the varied uses of the acronym STEM. From the emergence of STEM, there was both general and ambiguous use of the acronym. I viewed the situation as a good news, bad news scenario. The good news resided in greater recognition for science, technology, engineering, and mathematics in educational contexts. The bad news was confusion caused by the use of STEM for anything and everything vaguely related to one or combinations of the four disciplines.

At first, I shared the concerns of others about the meaning of STEM and the fact that it rapidly became one more educational slogan. And, the education community does not need another slogan. As I continued paying attention to the applications of STEM, I recognized its use as a general statement of goals: "We need more STEM majors." In other cases, STEM referred to schools: "There are STEM schools." And in others, STEM was a reference to school programs or practices: "We have a project-based STEM curriculum." Rather than joining the too often heard laments about the meaning of STEM, lack of a commonly shared national definition, or the acronym's ambiguity, I looked for meaningful and positive approaches to STEM, often revealed by listening or looking for the context within which individuals, groups, or reports used the acronym.

In time, I realized that listening for the context in which STEM was used usually revealed meaning and clarity. That said, there were still multiple ways the acronym was employed: reference to college majors, careers in business and industry, categories of economic growth, specialized schools, and a way to think about and organize the state, district, or school curriculum. Of all the references to STEM, the latter was, in my view, the least cited and the most needed.

Upon reading *STEM Lesson Essentials, Grades 3–8*, I had an immediate and positive response. Here was a team of authors who provided an antidote to those looking for definitions and clarifications—from a curriculum perspective. The authors of this book address the complex subject of STEM education with a work that is understandable and usable. They are clear about the audiences: teachers, curriculum specialists, and those providing professional development. They are clear about the limits of their subject: tools, models, and background for those interested in doing something about STEM.

The authors provide a much needed definition for those considering school programs. Here is their definition:

> STEM education is an interdisciplinary approach to learning which removes the traditional barriers separating the four disciplines of science, technology, engineering and mathematics, and integrates them into real world, rigorous and relevant learning experiences for students. (Chapter 1, p. 4)

From this point, the reader departs on a journey by answering fundamental questions about the nature and goals of STEM, providing guiding principles for effective STEM instruction, and describing curricular approaches to integrating STEM in classrooms.

The guiding principles provide a practical introduction and helpful orientation for those working on STEM programs. Here are the principles:

1. **Focus on Integration.** Combine two or more of the STEM disciplines so students can see the relationship among concepts.
2. **Establish Relevance.** Help the students develop meaning through the application of STEM knowledge.

3. **Emphasize Twenty-First-Century Skills.** Help students develop the knowledge and skills they need for the contemporary workforce.
4. **Challenge Your Students.** Provide projects, tasks, and activities that hold students' interest and challenge their understandings and abilities.
5. **Mix It Up.** Provide a variety of STEM lessons and activities for the students.

You can see from this list of guiding principles what the authors present for classroom teachers. Their ideas are informative and achievable. These are appropriate aims.

Each chapter begins by asking the reader to take a minute and reflect on the chapter's theme. The chapters are relatively short and conclude with reflections and references.

By not trying to write a STEM curriculum and thus recognizing the great diversity in states, districts, and schools, the authors move beyond the rhetoric and provide knowledge, tools, models, and examples that make STEM a reality of teaching and learning in classrooms.

STEM Lesson Essentials, Grades 3–8 is a decidedly positive addition to discussions of STEM education. The book moves discussion to where it should be—in schools, classrooms, and the hands of professional teachers.

—Rodger W. Bybee
Golden, Colorado
August 2012

CHAPTER 1

You May Already Be a STEM Teacher

What students learn about the science disciplines, technology, engineering, and mathematics during their K–12 schooling shapes their intellectual development, opportunities for future study and work, and choices of career, as well as their capacity to make informed decisions about political and civic issues and about their own lives. A wide array of public and personal issues—from global warming to medical treatment to social networking to home mortgages—involve science, technology, engineering, and mathematics (STEM). Indeed, the solutions to some of the most daunting problems facing the nation will require not only the expertise of top STEM professionals but also the wisdom and understanding of its citizens.

—*Successful STEM Education: A Workshop Summary*, National Research Council (2011, 1)

BEFORE YOU READ THIS CHAPTER, write down your own definition of STEM education.

Meet Stacey Greene

Stacey Greene is a fifth-grade teacher from Scottsdale, Arizona. Her capabilities as a teacher were recognized in 2006 when she received a Presidential Award for Mathematics and Science Teaching. She is also a National Board–certified teacher who has honed her craft through years of practice and taking advantage of many professional development opportunities. Stacey has been incorporating many of the tenets of STEM teaching in her classroom since long before it was actually called STEM. Here, in Stacey's words, is an experience she had with a parent who questioned her teaching.

Recently I had a mother come into my classroom and say, "My son says he is not doing math in math class." I was taken aback. No math in math class? Then I realized, this mom was expecting the usual worksheets with thirty division problems on them, or a list of numbers to find the mean, median, and mode, or a table of numbers to place onto a graph after they were told "Today is bar graph day" or "Today we are only making line graphs." It was then that I realized that I had to educate my parents about my method of STEM teaching.

Having a deep love for science teaching, I naturally begin with science as a springboard for learning and applying in a meaningful way the other STEM concepts we are learning in our curriculum. For example, in math we were studying data analysis and in science we were studying force and motion. Therefore, I joined the units together into a single series of classes about roller coasters.

On this particular day, the students designed roller coaster ramps and then timed a marble going down a ramp at one-second intervals. They then compiled their data onto one graph. Through this experiment they began to see that they were effectively measuring how quickly the marble was speeding up. Not only did they have to plot the data from seven groups on one graph, they had to decide what kind of graph to use (line or bar) and which data to use (mean, median, or mode).

I was feeling quite proud of my students: They had done data analysis using real data they obtained from an experiment that they had devised, made it meaningful by deciding the best way to utilize the data (mean, median, or mode), created a way to communicate the findings, and really understood how evidence is used to support a conclusion. All this without a worksheet of numbers to crunch, graphs to make with numbers that were irrelevant, and outliers that were just different but who knew why. Now I knew they understood these concepts because they had applied them in a meaningful way. Not to mention, I had a cool graph I could refer to throughout the school year to remind them of these concepts, and their understanding was enhanced.

STEM LESSON ESSENTIALS • Integrating Science, Technology, Engineering, and Mathematics

This was all well and good and the students were learning in a meaningful way but I now realize that this way of teaching means I have to educate my parents as well. I have to walk them through this type of experience so they can begin to see the interdisciplinary approach that I use to teach different concepts and that the students are not missing out on anything. In fact, my students score higher on tests than students in the other classrooms. I've realized that if we don't make learning meaningful and relevant to our students, then they will just learn the answer for the test and forget it after it is done.

I don't think I'm doing anything magical or radical. I believe that all of this is just good teaching. The subjects are meaningful, and the understanding deeper. Now that the time allocated for instruction in each subject adds up to more than the minutes students are in class, this type of relevant interdisciplinary teaching is essential for our students today. I hope other teachers will see how true STEM teaching and learning will actually make their lives easier once they have designed the lessons and units of study.

Stacey Greene has been a STEM teacher for a long time, although she has only recently been able to put a name to it as the idea of STEM teaching and learning has entered the mainstream. This is true of many elementary teachers who have naturally integrated the disciplines in self-contained classes. It is also true of many middle school teachers assigned to teach science, math, or technology but who recognize the value of crossing disciplinary boundaries. In fact, chances are that if you are reading this book, you are also a STEM teacher, at least some of the time.

STEM Teaching and Learning in Action

We will learn more about the details of this lesson in Chapter 4. From this quick overview, however, we can see how Stacey Greene is applying all four of the STEM subjects. The students used their *mathematics* knowledge and skills to measure distances, calculate speed, and plot data on a graph. They interpreted the graph using *science* concepts that describe motion in terms of distance, time, and speed, and they learned that an object increases its speed as it rolls downhill. To accomplish this, they had to become familiar with the lab *technology* (stopwatch, marble, ramp, and measuring tape). Finally, the students applied principles of *engineering* to create their own roller coaster. They also worked collaboratively, shared their information by communicating their results, and participated in class discourse. In other words, they participated in a STEM learning activity. Stacey used science as the content springboard for application of mathematics, technology, engineering, communication, and collaboration to design an interdisciplinary experience for her students.

STEM Education, an Operational Definition

We, the authors of this book, have agreed on a definition of STEM education. Through much discussion with professional colleagues from all over the country and with careful vetting for clarification and understanding, we offer this definition to help guide our discussion of STEM education in this book.

> STEM education is an interdisciplinary approach to learning that removes the traditional barriers separating the four disciplines of science, technology, engineering, and mathematics and integrates them into real-world, rigorous, and relevant learning experiences for students.

Unlike the well-trodden paths of mathematics and science teaching, STEM education is relatively new. For the past decade, we have been exploring this new frontier, and we don't claim to have all the answers. However, we believe we have learned enough to share our insights with you, the reader; and so we invite you to join us on our STEM journey. Here are some of the questions we will explore along the way:

- What is STEM teaching and learning? What does it look like in different classroom settings?
- What is STEM literacy?
- What are the different interdisciplinary levels of STEM teaching?
- How can an elementary teacher in a self-contained classroom begin to create STEM lessons and units?

- How can a content-specific teacher work with others to connect the STEM disciplines with each other and with language arts, social studies, art, and music?
- How will STEM help you do a better job of teaching the big ideas in the content areas and make the learning relevant for your students?
- How does STEM teaching and learning promote twenty-first-century skills?
- How can you help others in your district cross disciplinary boundaries to create a richer, more meaningful environment for students in your school and district?

Here is an overview of your STEM journey as you travel with us through this book:

Chapter 2 defines STEM literacy and explains why it's important for everyone to become STEM literate.

Chapter 3 lists the five guiding principles for effective STEM instruction: (1) focus on integration, (2) establish relevance, (3) emphasize twenty-first-century learning skills, (4) challenge your students, and (5) mix it up by providing a variety of instructional tasks and ways for your students to demonstrate their understanding.

Chapter 4 provides an example of what these principles look like in the hands of a master teacher.

Chapter 5 describes science and engineering practices as well as the practices in technology and mathematics. Figure 5.1 at the end of the chapter invites you to compare practices across the four fields to view their similarities and differences and see how they complement each other.

Chapter 6 describes an activity involving toy gears that is designed to engage students in guided activities in which they put practices to work in all four STEM fields.

Chapter 7 focuses on the two new partners to science and mathematics instruction—technology and engineering—and explains why they are important.

Chapter 8 describes three broad approaches to STEM education: *multidisciplinary*, in which teachers of several subjects coordinate their teaching to emphasize connections across the curriculum; *interdisciplinary* teaching, in which two or more subjects support each other; and *transdisciplinary*, that reflects students' interests and questions,

Chapters 9–11 give examples of what these levels of integration look like in the classroom. Chapter 9 describes what an interdisciplinary integrated science and mathematics lesson looks like at the elementary (3–5) grade level. Chapter 10 describes a middle school STEM unit that reflects all three integrated approaches, and Chapter 11 describes what these approaches look like from the perspective of a seventh-grade mathematics teacher.

Chapters 12–14 offer additional ideas for developing STEM lessons. Chapter 12 describes project-based learning, an especially powerful form of transdisciplinary instruction, and Chapter 13 offers suggestions for assessing integrated STEM units. Chapter 14 provides a template for getting started on planning a STEM lesson or unit and describes how the template was used to develop the Gears unit in Chapter 6.

Chapters 15 and 16 look at implementing STEM instruction at the school or district level. Chapter 15 provides an example of how a team of middle school teachers are applying these principles in the context of a unit of study that incorporates not only the four STEM fields but also language arts and social studies. Chapter 16 is a story of how an entire K–8 school district adopted an integrated STEM approach for all their students.

Chapter 17 provides a listing of other resources that go beyond this book to help you begin to implement STEM teaching in your classroom, school, or district.

Concluding Thoughts

Writing this book has engaged our thinking over the past year not only about where we want to go with STEM education but also about where we've been. Each of us has been a STEM teacher at some point in our careers, and these recollections helped us crystallize those ideas. In the following chapters, you'll hear about some of our teaching adventures and from others, like Stacey Greene, who blazed trails between and among the STEM fields long before STEM had a name, let alone a definition.

Reflection

- Compare your definition of STEM education with the operational definition given in this chapter. How is it similar? How is it different?

- Think back to Stacey's lesson example. Was there a time when you used a similar approach in your classroom or with other teachers?

- Are you a STEM teacher?

REFERENCE

National Research Council. 2011. *Successful STEM Education: A Workshop Summary*. A. Beatty, Rapporteur. Committee on Highly Successful Schools or Programs for K–12 STEM Education, Board on Science Education and Board on Testing and Assessment. Division of Behavioral and Social Sciences and Education. Washington, DC: The National Academies Press.

CHAPTER 2

STEM Literacy

BEFORE YOU READ THIS CHAPTER, write a few sentences to describe your vision of STEM literacy.

STEM education has many potential benefits for individuals and for the nation as a whole, Norman Augustine explained in an opening presentation. One factor that sets it apart from other branches of academic study for many policy makers is that literacy in STEM subjects is important both for the personal well-being of each citizen and for the nation's competitiveness in the global economy.

—Successful STEM Education: A Workshop Summary, National Research Council (2011, 3)

Origin of the Term STEM

The term *STEM* is now widely used across the United States and around the world, but what does it mean and how is STEM education different from the traditional mathematics and science disciplines? To answer this, we begin with a brief historical perspective on the acronym *STEM* and how it came to be used.

The term *STEM* was originally used at the National Science Foundation (NSF) to be inclusive of all their education-related programs across NSF's different agencies. Today, that acronym is widely used in many different contexts and has come to be recognized as a meta-discipline—an integration of formerly separate subjects into a new and coherent field of study. For example, the relatively new field of biotechnology is the crossroads of the studies of biology, which involves the study of living organisms and their processes, with the applications of engineering and design to create new products or processes. This type of education involves the "creation of a discipline based on the integration of other disciplinary knowledge into a new 'whole.' This interdisciplinary bridging among discrete disciplines is now treated as an entity, known as STEM" (Morrison 2006, 4).

The *T* and the *E*

The *T* and the *E* in *STEM* are often overlooked because traditionally, only science and mathematics have been included in the school curriculum. Also, many people believe that "technology" only refers to devices "with a plug," including computers and other high-tech tools, where in reality it denotes a much broader and deeper array of products, processes, and systems. The term *engineering* is also poorly understood, with some people considering it to be just for "whiz kids" who shine at math and science, and others think it is "a vocational subject" like plumbing and automotive repair. In fact, science, technology, engineering, and mathematics each have a unique body of established knowledge and practices that are important for every citizen in the twenty-first century. Taken together, the combination of these individual disciplines into a new whole introduces the notion of "STEM literacy," which we describe in this chapter.

What Is STEM Literacy?

The main goal of STEM education is not for students to become mathematicians, scientists, technicians, or engineers; although it would be great if more of our youth had such aspirations. The goal is for all students to be able to function and thrive in our highly technological world—that is, to be STEM literate. *Stem literacy* as defined by the National Research Council's recent report *Successful K–12 STEM Education: Identifying Effective Approaches in Science, Technology,*

Engineering and Mathematics, is "the knowledge and understanding of scientific and mathematical concepts and processes required of personal decision making, participation in civic and cultural affairs and economic productivity" (National Research Council 2011, 5).

STEM literacy weaves together these four interrelated capabilities:

- *Scientific literacy* is defined by the National Research Council (2012) as consisting of three dimensions: (1) knowledge of the key facts, concepts, principles, laws, and theories in the science disciplines; (2) the ability to connect these ideas across disciplines; and (3) practices and ways of thinking that advance our knowledge of the natural world, as well as the use of science to solve real-world problems through engineering.

- *Technological literacy* is "the ability to use, manage, understand, and assess technology" (International Technology and Engineering Education Association 2007, 7), and *technology* is defined as "any modification of the natural world made to fulfill human needs or desires" (National Research Council 2012, 202). Technologies range from the simplest artifacts, such as paper and pencil, to the most complex systems, including buildings and cities, the electric power grid, satellites, and the Internet. "Furthermore, technology includes the entire infrastructure needed to design, manufacture, operate, and repair these technological artifacts" (National Assessment Governing Board 2011, xi). "Students should know how to use new technologies, understand how new technologies are developed, and have skills to analyze how new technologies affect us, our nation, and the world" (National Governor's Association 2007, 7).

- *Engineering literacy* is the ability to solve problems and accomplish goals by applying the engineering design process—a systematic and often iterative approach to designing objects, processes, and systems to meet human needs and wants. Students able to apply the practices of engineering to new situations know how to define a solvable problem, are able to generate and test potential solutions, and know how to modify the design in making trade-offs among multiple considerations (e.g., functional, ethical, economic, aesthetic) to reach an optimal solution. Engineering literacy involves recognition of the mutually supportive relationship between the sciences, arts, and engineering, as well as the ways in which engineers respond to the interests and needs of society, which in turn affect society and the environment by bringing about technological change (National Assessment Governing Board 2011, xi, 1–4; National Research Council 2012, 202).[1]

- *Mathematical literacy* is "an individual's capacity to identify and understand the role that mathematics plays in the world. Students who are mathematically literate are able to make well-founded judgments and to use and engage with mathematics in ways that meet the needs of that individual's life as a constructive, concerned and reflective citizen" (Organisation for Economic Co-operation and Development 2009, 15). A mathematically literate person is able to express mathematical ideas in words, to participate in discussions about mathematics, and to apply the concepts and skills of mathematics to everyday life.

An important quality of STEM literacy is that there is no set threshold to separate those who are STEM literate and those who are not. Like language literacy, it continues to grow and develop throughout a person's lifetime as they improve their abilities and skills to write in different styles and to read in different genres.

The same holds true for STEM teaching and learning development. STEM literacy also grows throughout a person's lifetime as they add to and improve their knowledge of the STEM fields, better understand their interconnections,

---

[1] The *Technology and Engineering Literacy Framework for the 2014 National Assessment of Educational Progress* (National Assessment Governing Board 2011) provides a single definition of *technology and engineering literacy*. We find it more useful to distinguish between *technology* and *engineering literacy* for the purposes of improving curriculum, instruction, and assessment. The definition of *engineering literacy* in this paragraph is synthesized from both the 2014 National Assessment of Educational Progress Framework and the National Research Council 2012 Framework.

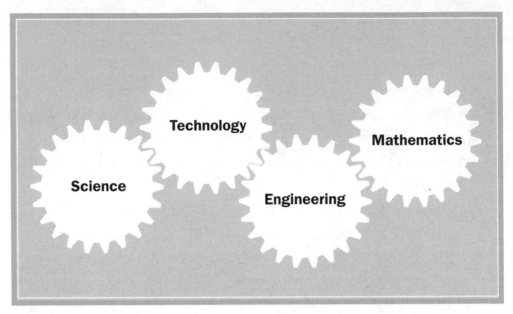

Figure 2.1 Like the meshing of teeth on a system of gears, the four STEM fields are best taught, learned, and assessed together.

and learn to apply that knowledge to answer questions and solve problems of interest to them. Therefore, as you improve your level of STEM teaching knowledge, it will be reflected in what you are able to do in the classroom.

It is important to emphasize, however, that these are not four separate capabilities, but represent abilities that are intertwined and overlapping. As we will illustrate in this book, like the meshing of teeth on a system of gears, these four capabilities are interconnected and often drive each other forward. Consequently, they are best taught, learned, and assessed together whenever possible.

STEM Viewed Holistically

We end this chapter by noting that STEM education is not fundamentally different from other teaching and learning, except that we are asking students to make additional connections, not only between the STEM subjects but also with other knowledge, ideas, and concerns that they bring into the classroom. Consequently, the ideas in this book build on but do not replace prior insights into the practices of effective teaching and learning.

An especially useful perspective on teaching and learning is described in an influential report from the National Research Council, *How People Learn: Brain, Mind, Experience, and School* (1999), which summarized the results of thirty years of research on learning and teaching. Many of the research findings were summed up as four interconnected "environments" that mutually support one another: learner-centered, knowledge-centered, and assessment-centered environments, and the broader community (Bransford et al. 1999, 121–22).

- A **knowledge-centered** learning environment is based on an analysis of what we want students to know and be able to do as a result of the learning experience and helps students develop the foundational and enduring knowledge, skills, and attitudes needed for successful transfer of this knowledge.
- A **learner-centered** environment connects the strengths, interests, and preconceptions of learners to their current academic tasks and learning goals and helps students learn about themselves as learners.
- An **assessment-centered** environment provides multiple opportunities to monitor and make visible students' progress in revising their thinking and applying their growing knowledge to new situations and tasks.
- All learning takes place within a **community**, including the community of the classroom, the school, and the neighborhood where the student lives. It is important for teachers to take into account the social norms and expectations that are imposed by each of these communities.

As described in Chapter 6 of the National Research Council report (1999), these four environments are to be envisioned holistically, rather than in bits and pieces. Similarly, we propose that the four STEM fields are best taught, learned, and assessed holistically, rather than as separate, unrelated subjects.

Concluding Thoughts

STEM is not a "new" subject in the sense that the capabilities now encompassed by the term have been a part of mainstream educational goals for decades. By emphasizing the four STEM "literacies," we promote the idea that STEM is not a single subject that replaced several others. Students still need to learn the same concepts and skills in science and mathematics as they did before; and they need to understand and be able to use many different types of technologies and how to solve problems through engineering design. On the other hand, by linking these four school subjects and planning to teach them holistically, we have the opportunity to provide more meaningful and motivating lessons.

Reflection

- Compare your vision of STEM literacy before reading this chapter with the vision of STEM literacy described in this chapter. How are they similar? How are they different?

- How might you apply the concept of STEM literacy to your own teaching?

- Why do you think the chapter ends with a holistic vision of the classroom?

REFERENCES

International Technology and Engineering Education Association. 2007. *Standards for Technological Literacy: Content for the Study of Technology*. International Technology and Engineering Education Association. Reston, VA: ITEEA.

Morrison, Janice S. 2006. The STEM Education Monograph Series, Attributes of STEM Education, The Student, The School, The Classroom. Baltimore, MD: Teaching Institute for Excellence in STEM.

National Assessment Governing Board. 2010. *Technology and Engineering Literacy Framework for the 2014 National Assessment of Educational Progress*. Available at: www.nagb.org/publications/frameworks/prepub_naep_tel_framework_2014.pdf.

National Research Council. 1999. *How People Learn: Brain, Mind, Experience, and School*. Washington, DC: National Academy Press.

———. 2011. *Successful STEM Education: A Workshop Summary*. A. Beatty, Rapporteur. Committee on Highly Successful Schools or Programs for K–12 STEM Education, Board on Science Education and Board on Testing and Assessment. Division of Behavioral and Social Sciences and Education. Washington, DC: The National Academies Press.

———. 2012. *A Framework for K–12 Science Education: Practices, Crosscutting Concepts, and Core Ideas.* Committee on a Conceptual Framework for New K–12 Science Education Standards. Board on Science Education, Division of Behavioral and Social Sciences and Education. Washington, DC: The National Academy Press. Available at: http://www.nap.edu/catalog.php?record_id=13165.

Organisation for Economic Co-operation and Development. 2009. *Mathematical Literacy: Programme for International Student Assessment (PISA) Assessment Framework.*

3

Guiding Principles

In the 21st century, scientific and technological innovations have become increasingly important as we face the benefits and challenges of both globalization and a knowledge-based economy. To succeed in this new information-based and highly technological society, all students need to develop their capabilities in science, technology, engineering and mathematics (STEM) to levels much beyond what was considered acceptable in the past.

—National Science Board, National Action Plan for STEM Education (October, 2007)

Being Intentional About STEM

Traditionally, only two of the four STEM fields have been included in the educational curriculum for all students: science and mathematics. Although there have been many attempts to bring these two fields together, they are nearly always taught separately. So it may seem odd at first that introducing two additional disciplines—technology and engineering—can achieve the goal of an integrated STEM curriculum. But as we will show in this book, the addition of technology and engineering can make the traditional math or science lesson come alive for your students.

First, however, it is important to clarify that we are not proposing adding two more subjects to the school curriculum. To the contrary, we propose integrating the technology and engineering practices into existing mathematics and science lessons and, on occasion, into the social studies and language arts lessons as well. Also, we are not advocating that all four STEM disciplines be integrated together in every unit. In many cases combining just two or three of the four disciplines can enrich a unit and provide a more rewarding student experience. It's the *connection* between disciplines that is important and the opportunities that students have to deepen their conceptual understandings while at the same time honing their skills by applying what they have learned in new contexts or in different settings.

What is most important is to be intentional when fusing one discipline to another. Although many instructional units already combine two or more of the STEM areas, the shift in disciplines is rarely pointed out, so that many teaching opportunities are missed. In this book we will point out when the shifts occur and what students are expected to learn from each discipline. This means that as teachers, it is important to be keenly aware of the distinctions among the four disciplines, so that you can weave them together in meaningful ways for your students.

It is also important to remember that STEM in itself is not a curriculum, but rather a way of organizing and delivering instruction. It is not another "ingredient" in the lesson soup, but a recipe for helping learners apply their knowledge, work together with their peers, and see the relevance in what they are learning. To better understand how to weave these disciplines together, we have established a set of STEM Guiding Principles, which we feel will provide some guidance to the process of creating these integrated units. These overarching principles can be thought of as suggestions for measuring, combining, and cooking the ingredients in the recipe to refashion the "silo approach" to our traditional units of study.

STEM Guiding Principles

1. **Focus on Integration:** Combining two or more of the disciplines allows you to help students see the relatedness of the concepts, tying together seemingly disjointed blocks of information. Whether you are combining science and engineering, two fields of science, or social studies and math, an interdisciplinary approach will help your students forge connections among concepts in their knowledge base, generate more innovative and creative solutions when considering opportunities to apply their understandings, and think more broadly about a given problem or situation.

2. **Establish Relevance:** It is not always apparent to the students how or when new learning will be applicable, so it is important to convey how this knowledge will be useful. Consider the following questions from the students' point of view. Why should I care about this? Does it address a real-world problem or current event situation? Is there some local or global issue or event that would make this appealing to know more about? Is there a real-world work or career opportunity that would be interesting for me to consider? Can I get a better job if I know about this or develop this skill?

3. **Emphasize Twenty-First-Century Skills:** The critical need for the workforce of tomorrow is not how much knowledge the citizens possess but how they can access information when needed and how they use that information to creatively solve problems and communicate ideas and concepts effectively. Teamwork and collaboration, along with critical thinking, problem solving, creativity, and communication—collectively known as "twenty-first-century skills"—will be the desirable attributes of tomorrow's workers (Partnership for 21st Century Skills 2009).

4. **Challenge Your Students:** By using grade-level-appropriate challenges, students are more apt to be intrigued with the work and not suffer from boredom. It is important to plan tasks that are not so difficult that students give up, nor so easy that students find the work boring. Emphasis on

twenty-first-century skills allows for a greater range of participation from all students—not just those who have the content knowledge expertise.

5. **Mix It Up:** By providing a variety of outcomes in STEM units of study, students are regularly presented with ways to express their knowledge, share their expertise, and expand their skill set. It is important to include both *problem-based* approaches (tasks in which students are given a particular problem to solve, which requires a creative solution) and *project-based* approaches (where students have significant control over what they wish to produce, how they want to demonstrate their learning, and in some cases, how they wish to be evaluated).

Concluding Thoughts

These five principles are certainly not the only ones that may be useful in developing STEM lessons and units. However, they are ideas that we have found useful over the past twelve months as we examined our own thinking in creating this book. As you develop your own STEM lessons or reflect on those that you've developed in the past, feel free to add principles that will help you move toward the goals that you consider the most important.

In the next chapter, we will explore how the STEM Guiding Principles function in a real fifth-grade classroom.

Reflection

- Is STEM a curriculum? A strategy? A goal? How would you support your answer?

- What would you consider to be the major goal of STEM education?

- How can STEM teaching provide learning opportunities that are different from the traditional approach?

- Which of the Guiding Principles do you already use in your own teaching? Which do you intend to use in the future?

REFERENCES

National Science Foundation. 1996. *Shaping the Future: New Expectations for Undergraduate Education in Science, Mathematics, Engineering, and Technology.* Arlington, VA: Director of Education and Human Resources, National Science Foundation. Available at: http://serc .carleton.edu/resources/1437.html.

National Research Council. 1999. *How People Learn: Brain, Mind, Experience, and School.* Washington, DC: National Academy Press. Available at: http://www.nap.edu/catalog .php?record_id=9853.

National Science Board. 2007. A National Action Plan for Addressing the Critical Needs for the U.S. Science, Technology, Engineering, and Mathematics Education System. October, 2007.Washington, DC. Available at: http://www.nsf.gov/nsb/documents/2007/stem_action.pdf.

National Science Foundation. 2006. Investing in America's Future, NSF Strategic Plan FY 2006–2011. Available at: http://www.nsf.gov/pubs/2006/nsf0648/NSF-06-48.pdf.

Partnership for 21st Century Skills. 2009. 21st Century Skills Maps. Available at: http://science.nsta.org/ps/Final21stCSkillsMapScience.pdf.

An Approach That Came Naturally

The framework is motivated in part by a growing national consensus around the need for greater coherence—that is, a sense of unity—in K–12 science education. Too often, standards are long lists of detailed and disconnected facts, reinforcing the criticism that science curricula in the United States tend to be "a mile wide and an inch deep." Not only is such an approach alienating to young people, but it can also leave them with just fragments of knowledge and little sense of the creative achievements of science, its inherent logic and consistency, and its universality. Moreover, that approach neglects the need for students to develop an understanding of the practices of science and engineering, which is as important to understanding science as knowledge of its content.

—A Framework for K–12 Science Education: Practices, Crosscutting Concepts, and Core Ideas,
National Research Council (2012, 10)

BEFORE READING THIS CHAPTER, reflect on your own teaching practices. To what extent is your overall teaching plan coherent? Are students able to see the connections among the various concepts and skills they are learning?

Moving Beyond the Acronym

By now you may be thinking, "Oh my, this all sounds good in theory but how am I going to do all of this in my classroom?" Time is short; time to plan is even shorter! So please just remember you don't have to do it all.

You can begin by focusing on one or a few guiding principles as you move into a more interdisciplinary, integrated approach to your teaching.

If STEM education is going to advance beyond the acronym, we will have to describe what it looks like in the classroom. So to that end, we will turn to a more detailed description of what STEM looks like when presented by a master teacher.

We met Stacey Greene in Chapter 1, where she talked about how a parent thought her son was not doing math in math class and how Stacey had to educate her students' parents about her classroom practices. She is one of those teachers who had been doing integrated, interdisciplinary teaching but did not have a word (or acronym) for what she was doing. To her, it was an approach that came naturally. In this chapter, Stacey illustrates the STEM guiding principles by sharing the thinking that led her to develop a Roller-Coaster math unit.

Guiding Principle 1: Focus on Integration

I have always realized that math out of context of the real world does not create curiosity or build conceptual understanding like it does when taught in conjunction with science and engineering. Given that I had a gifted fifth-grade math class and they were learning simple machines in science in their regular classroom, I looked at various technologies that integrated simple machines and that would have high interest for the students. Roller coasters are a favorite of mine and I realized that through them the students could apply the concepts of force, motion, speed, and acceleration, constructing models, and analyzing patterns and relationships. Plus, students could apply engineering— ask, imagine, plan, create, and test—to design and improve the model. With all of this rich content it all just began to take shape.

Stacey's thinking here illuminates Guiding Principle 1, that combining two or more of the disciplines helps students see the relatedness of the concepts, tying together seemingly disjointed blocks of information. In this case, Stacey's students will be using their math skills in a real-life context. Her goal is not just for the students to learn to "do the math," but to also recognize that the math

STEM LESSON ESSENTIALS • Integrating Science, Technology, Engineering, and Mathematics

they are learning can be a fundamental tool to accomplish something of interest to them.

Guiding Principle 2: Establish Relevance

The overall plan for the Roller-Coaster unit also embodied Guiding Principle 2, to establish relevance. From the students' point of view, the goal was to design and build a roller coaster using a flexible track—a fun activity for fifth graders. To reach their goal, the teacher explained that students first needed to learn a little more about how a marble moved along the track, so they would need to start with a simple straight track and see what happened to the marble.

In this lesson, the students were given a metric measuring tape, marbles, masking tape, three sections of plastic track, and meter sticks to use as straight flat boards to stabilize the track. In their groups, they were to design a marble run with the track and marble as constants. Students attached one end of the track to the wall at a height of about ten to fifteen centimeters, and experimented with the height until the marble rolled down the ramp in as close to three seconds as possible. (I don't tell them exactly how high to tape the ramp to the wall because that would not require them to think. It's also more interesting to analyze the data if there is a range of different measurements.)

Once the students had taped their meter sticks to the wall at the right height, they laid the metric measuring tape along the track so they could measure distance in centimeters and practice using their stopwatches. When they were ready, they released the marble at the top of the ramp and marked the distance traveled after one second, two seconds, and three seconds. The teams conducted three trials and wrote the results in a table. (The arrangement of lab materials for this activity is shown in Figure 4.1.)

Because each group was allowed to plan and conduct the experiment without detailed instructions, they had difficulty keeping the release, markings, and timing constant. They discussed how to improve their methods, and most of the groups eventually determined it was best if each person did the same job throughout the experiment, so that any errors in timing or measuring were consistent.

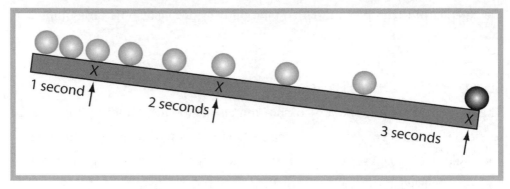

Figure 4.1 Students marked the position of the marble after one, two, and three seconds.

Guiding Principle 3: Emphasize Twenty-First-Century Skills

Stacey has her students work in groups whenever possible. Sometimes she assigns them to their learning group because she wants students of different abilities working together. At other times she lets them select their partners. Providing a structure and incentives for students to work in groups is not just for convenience or to make it more fun, but to provide an opportunity for students to increase their skills in communication and collaboration—two of the twenty-first-century skills included in Guiding Principle 3.

> The students used the formula S = D/T (speed equals distance divided by time) to calculate the average speed of the marble during the first, second, and third second on the ramp. As a class we discussed the findings—"Was the marble's speed constant in each second, or did the speed change?" The students were able to articulate in their own words that the marble went faster each second, and so we defined that kind of motion as acceleration. We also discussed what force might be causing the acceleration.
>
> I should mention that this definition of acceleration (speeding up) was not the complete use of the term (we did not include slowing down or change in direction). They used the term acceleration in their discussions with this more simplified understanding that is developmentally appropriate for fifth graders' understanding and experience. I have found that having a concept that is accurate but a partial understanding can be useful for building further conceptual depth later.

STEM LESSON ESSENTIALS • Integrating Science, Technology, Engineering, and Mathematics

Next we decided to create a large graph with all of the group's data included. Each group plotted three points: the distance the marble moved at one second, the distance at two seconds, and the distance at three seconds (using the averages of their three trials). On the graph the x-axis represented time and the y-axis represented the distance that the marble traveled. When all the data were marked on the graph, the results were surprising. Although most of the group's points were clustered together on the graph, one set was clearly different from the others. A heated discussion ensued about why this outlier happened, and if these data were valid.

Once we had determined in class the cause for the outlier data (one group had chosen a lower incline for their design; something that would not have happened had I not let them do the design themselves), they decided to ignore the outlier data for the purposes of creating the line graph.

Allowing the students to debate, discuss, and support their claims took quite a bit of time, but it was worth it. What this lively discussion gave me, as the teacher, was an opportunity to facilitate a discussion of outliers in a way that they understood and was in context of something they had done. This had been a difficult concept for my students to see as important during our math lessons when they had just been given data on the worksheets that had outliers. They just treated them as the book said they must in math. But now, they had a lively debate on how they could use these data and what they meant. On their own, students came to agreement that scientists and engineers cannot automatically reject outlier data as due to human error, since it may sometimes be a real effect worthy of further study.

Guiding Principle 4: Challenge Your Students

Stacey's teaching embodies Guiding Principle 4, to challenge students, in a number of ways. She introduced the term *acceleration*, which the students will not see in a formal way until late in middle school. She purposely limited the instructions she provided so the students would have to figure out the best way to conduct their research. Finally, when a question about outliers came up, she did not solve the problem for the students—she made them do the work of figuring out what may have caused the outliers and what to do about it.

This was but one set of lessons in this unit about motion. From this experience and others within this unit, they were ultimately able to use these acceleration models to engineer their own roller coaster and made inclines that gave the marble enough acceleration to make it up the next hill or through a loop. But one of the unplanned benefits of this set of lessons was the graph we had. I kept it all year, and we referred to it often when discussing data, analyzing data, and trying to relate concepts. And the best part was, we had done not one worksheet, yet they understood mathematical relationships between variables, how to analyze data in the most meaningful way to support their conclusion, and what an outlier truly was. By having my students recognize and apply what they had been learning in science and math, they were able to engage in analyzing their data, evaluating results, and arguing from evidence.

Guiding Principle 5: Mix It Up

As described earlier, Stacey's students needed to solve a number of different problems. They needed to work as a team to design their experiment so as to get consistent data. When they ran into a problem—what to do with anomalous data—they had to figure out what to do about it. In the culminating part of the unit they engaged in an engineering design activity, also characterized as "project-based" learning, in which there were many possible answers. They demonstrated their understanding of various concepts and skills in mathematics and science throughout the design process, and when presenting their ideas at the conclusion of the unit.

> For the culminating activity, I put students into teams to design and build their own roller coasters using the knowledge and skills they had learned through this unit about motion and forces. Most of them wanted to build a roller coaster that would allow the marble to travel the greatest distance in the shortest amount of time. However, I asked them to first develop their design blueprint. During this experience, they negotiated with one another about what the roller coaster would look like and what materials they were going to use in its construction. Once they developed their design, they then used materials I had put out for them: masking tape, string, plastic tracks, rulers, meter sticks,

tubes, cardboard boxes, heavy paper, and so on. After sawing, taping, painting, and experimenting were complete, most of the roller coasters stood over five feet tall. They incorporated loops, elevator mechanisms, pulleys, inclined planes, and more. As their blueprints became three-dimensional, the students had to test each aspect of the design and adjust it so the marble would continue through the entire roller coaster. One group spent three days and many trials getting their elevator mechanism to work. They also made many adjustments on the loops so that the marble would consistently move through the loop and continue on.

The students referred back to the graphs we had made of speed and velocity. They used the knowledge of how the marble speeds up faster and faster as it rolls farther downhill. They found they needed to remember concepts and ideas from our experiments with friction that we had done earlier and they discovered more complex examples of acceleration. They also recalled how to place and release the marble so it behaved consistently each time.

It was a glorious experience for my students and for me. We invited the principal and other classes to see the roller coasters in action. And of course I was not going to let all their hard work go to waste, so on parents' night the students demonstrated their roller coasters and explained what they had learned in designing them about science, mathematics, and engineering.

You have seen how Stacey Greene quite naturally took to STEM teaching. When we asked her if this was difficult, she replied, "Actually, I had been doing much of this type of teaching for years because it was a lot more fun to teach this way, and I think my students got a lot out of it. However, I don't think I fully realized that I was a STEM teacher until I heard about the definition of STEM education and the guiding principles. Now my goal is helping mentor others on how easy it really can be."

Concluding Thoughts

One of the goals of Stacey's teaching was to help students recognize that mathematics is a fundamental tool for representing physical relationships. In this case, for example, the concept of speed is a mathematical relationship between time and the distance traveled during that time. The concept of acceleration is an even more complex idea involving the change in speed over time. The idea that mathematics is a powerful tool for understanding the physical world is yet another fundamental concept in STEM teaching. Although this idea is challenging, it is not too advanced for elementary students, beginning perhaps with the idea that a number represents a collection of objects—no matter what the objects may be (Standards of Mathematical Practice #2, CCSS).

Reflection

- Describe a time in your own experience when you have had an opportunity to apply mathematics in your science lessons or science in your mathematics lessons. Do you think the students recognized how closely these subjects are related?

- Think about the sequence of activities described in this chapter. Why was it necessary for the students to investigate the speed of a marble rolling down a ramp before designing their roller coasters? Do you think the students saw it the same way the teacher did?

- In your opinion, what were the key steps that Stacey took to help the students succeed?

REFERENCES

Common Core State Standards Initiative. Mathematics. 2010. National Governors Association Center for Best Practices and Council of Chief State School Officers. Available at: www.corestandards.org/the-standards/mathematics/.

National Research Council. 2012. *A Framework for K–12 Science Education: Practices, Crosscutting Concepts, and Core Ideas.* Committee on New Science Education Standards, Board on Science Education, Division of Behavioral and Social Sciences and Education. Washington, DC: National Academy Press. Available at: http://www.nap.edu/catalog.php?record_id=13165.

CHAPTER 5

What Are the STEM Practices?

Today, it is widely accepted that "STEM education is an interdisciplinary approach to learning where rigorous academic concepts are coupled with real-world, relevant lessons. Students can apply science, technology, engineering, and mathematics in contexts that help them make connections between school, community, work, and the global enterprise. This enables the development of STEM literacy and with it the ability to compete in the new economy."

—STEM Education: A Project to Identify the Missing Components, Tsupros, Kohler, and Hallinen (2009)

BEFORE READING THIS CHAPTER, take a moment to reflect on the four disciplines found in STEM and then jot down what you think they might all have in common. For example, do they all promote questioning and problem solving?

From Process to Practice

A new vision is emerging about the nature of science as it should be practiced in the classroom. Most teachers are aware that science is more than a body of facts; and for at least the last fifteen years, since publication of *Benchmarks for Science Literacy* (American Association for the Advancement of Science 1993) and the *National Science Education Standards* (National Research Council [NRC] 1996), emphasis has been on the processes of scientific inquiry, such as observing, investigating, collecting data, and drawing conclusions.

In an effort to revise the earlier standards and provide a blueprint for states to collaborate and adopt common standards in science, in 2012 the NRC published a new guide to what all students should know and be able to do. *A Framework for K–12 Science Education: Practices, Crosscutting Concepts, and Core Ideas* (NRC 2012) takes the position that inquiry processes are not sufficient. Students should also know how to apply what they learn in practical situations that they might encounter in everyday life. To emphasize the practical nature of these capabilities, the *Framework* uses the term *science and engineering practices* rather than *processes*. And because the practices of science and engineering are similar but not the same, the *Framework* presents them side by side. (The following statements are drawn from NRC 2012, Box 3-2, pages 50–55. The full text is available at www.nap.edu/catalog.php?record_id=13165.)

Science and Engineering Practices

Practice 1: Ask questions and define problems. *Science* begins with a question about a natural phenomenon and seeks to develop testable answers to such questions. *Engineering* begins with a problem, need, or desire and creates questions to better define the problem, determine criteria for a successful solution, and identify any constraints, parameters, or limitations that need to be considered.

Practice 2: Develop and use models. *Science* often involves the construction and use of models and simulations to help make predictions that can be tested and to develop explanations about natural phenomena. *Engineering* makes use of models and simulations to analyze existing systems, explore modifications, and test proposed solutions.

Practice 3: Plan and carry out investigations. In science, investigations are planned to answer the testable question, determine the procedures, identify the variables, define the conditions to be examined, and determine how the results will be recorded. Engineers plan investigations to learn more about the problem to be solved, identify factors that can impact results, and test possible solutions. They consider altering conditions to maximize improvements to meet the criteria and constraints within the scope of the defined problem.

Practice 4: Analyze and interpret data. Both scientists and engineers use a range of tools—including tables, graphs, diagrams, and statistical analyses—to identify the significant features and patterns in the data gathered from their investigations.

Practice 5: Use mathematics and computational thinking. Both scientists and engineers use mathematics and computation as fundamental tools for representing physical variables and their relationships and for a range of tasks, such as constructing simulations and recording and analyzing data.

Practice 6: Construct explanations and design solutions. In *science*, the goal is to construct explanations that reflect the findings of the investigation. In *engineering*, the goal is to propose solutions (sometimes multiple solution scenarios) to the identified problem, satisfying different constraints or criteria.

Practice 7: Engage in argument from evidence. In *science*, reasoning and argument are essential for finding the best explanation for a natural phenomenon. In *engineering*, reasoning and argument are used to defend the best possible solution to a problem. Engineers use systematic methods to compare alternative solutions, trading off one feature for another to optimize solutions.

Practice 8: Obtain, evaluate, and communicate information. Both scientists and engineers must be able to communicate their findings clearly and persuasively, either orally or in writing, with the use of tables, diagrams, graphs, and equations. Both require the ability to derive meaning from scientific texts (such as papers, the Internet, symposia, and lectures), to evaluate the validity of the information from these sources, and to integrate that information into their findings.

Technology Practices

To appreciate how thoroughly technologies pervade our lives, try the thought experiment shown in Figure 5.1.

Figure 5.1 Thought experiment.

A Thought Experiment About Technology

Imagine that all of the technologies around you were to disappear. What would be missing from your life right now? What would you see? How would your life be different? Take a minute and jot down your ideas, then read on to see how others have responded to this question.

Responses to the Thought Experiment

"My computer will disappear. I guess I don't have to answer email today."

"Hey, my cell phone just disappeared."

"The electricity went out too—no more lights, no air conditioning."

"Actually this entire building has been designed and built to provide shelter. So I guess the whole building is gone."

"What about the plants? They're natural, aren't they?"

"No, not really. Most are species from other places that were carried here on ships and planes. Others are modified by selective breeding or grafting."

"Hmmm, what happened to my clothes? They're made out of natural fibers!"

"Maybe so, but weaving and knitting are technologies."

"So, here we are. No clothes and surrounded by trees because we have no axes to cut them down. How do we eat? Hmm, maybe those squirrels have some ideas. . . ."

As explained in Chapter 2, *technology* in a broad sense is defined as any modification of the natural world done to fulfill human needs or desires. However, that brief definition does not do justice to the full breadth of technological systems that make up our world. Think of the global transportation system that includes hundreds of thousands of airplanes and ships and hundreds of millions of cars, motorcycles, and bikes. Or, consider the global system for

STEM LESSON ESSENTIALS • Integrating Science, Technology, Engineering, and Mathematics

growing, processing, and transporting food, or the system of medical care that includes hospitals, doctors, nurses, medical schools, medical equipment suppliers, pharmaceutical companies, drugstores, medical insurance companies, and professional organizations for the people who work in different sectors of the medical economy. Equally complex are systems for transporting, purifying, and distributing clean water, producing usable energy from natural resources, building cities and towns, and so forth.

The NRC's *Framework* (2012) does not identify "technology practices." However, it clearly defines *technology* broadly, and several of the core ideas that all students should learn involve technology. Following is a set of four essential practices that we have drawn from the *Framework* and other related materials that we believe are consistent and parallel to the "science and engineering practices" that are identified in Chapter 3 of the *Framework*.

> **Practice 1: Become aware of the web of technological systems on which society depends.** When most people think about *technology*, they generally envision computers or other digital tools. However, it is important that we enable our students to think more broadly and become aware of the vast number of interrelated technologies around them. Reflection is the key here, as it is important for students to start with aspects of the world that are familiar and to recognize that if they were created by people, to serve human needs and desires, then they are *technologies*. Activities like the thought experiment described previously can help students begin to see the technologies that surround them, but it may take a variety of different activities for students to appreciate the full complexities of technological systems.
>
> **Practice 2: Learn how to use new technologies as they become available.** *Technology education* in schools today usually refers to teaching students how to use computers for all sorts of different purposes, from finding and vetting sources of information, to using computers much as scientists do, to make measurements, collect data, and immediately represent and display information in multiple graphic formats. However, an essential characteristic of technology is that it is always changing, so that learning

to use today's tools is not sufficient. We cannot fully prepare students to engage in tomorrow's technologies because we don't know what these technologies will be. To equip our students to adjust to a world of changing technologies, we need to help them learn how to learn new technologies, to choose the technology that is most appropriate for a given task, to examine ways that others have used the technology, to start with simple tasks and apply the technology to progressively more complex tasks, to take advantage of tutorials and manuals, and so on.

Practice 3: Recognize the role that technology plays in the advancement of science and engineering. The role of technology in advancing science is well known through stories in the history of science. For example, Galileo would not have observed mountains and craters on the Moon without the telescope. Similarly, today's astronomers depend on advanced technologies like the Hubble Space Telescope, and medical researchers employ genetic engineering to create new medicines. The engineers who design these technological devices, systems, and processes are equally important in advancing our knowledge of the natural world as the scientists who use them. Science also helps to advance the work of engineers. Aerospace engineers apply the discoveries of Newton and Einstein to launch satellites into space, and materials engineers apply their knowledge of chemistry to create concrete and steel with properties needed to build modern highways and skyscrapers. In other words, engineers design the technologies that scientists use to advance science, and scientists provide engineers with knowledge of the natural world they need to design new technologies.

Practice 4: Make informed decisions about technology, given its relationship to society and the environment. From the invention of stone tools and fire, technological changes have brought about changes in the way people live. These changes have accelerated in recent decades, as the development of airplanes, cell phones, and computers have brought people together in ways never possible before. Similarly, technological developments have impacted the environment as farms, factories, and cities have displaced forests and wetlands. As human populations have grown, the impacts on the global environment have increased. Consequently, it is important for everyone to recognize both the positive and negative consequences of technological decisions and to make informed decisions. This idea was captured in a statement by the National Academy of Engineering in their report, *Technically Speaking: Why All Americans Need to Know More About Technology*.

> As far into the future as our imaginations take us, we will face challenges that depend on the development and application of technology. Better health, more abundant food, more humane living and working conditions, cleaner air and water, more effective education, and scores of other improvements in the human condition are within our grasp. But none of these improvements are guaranteed, and many problems will arise that we cannot predict. To take full advantage of the benefits and to recognize, address, or even avoid the pitfalls of technology, Americans must become better stewards of technological change. (Pearson et al. 2002, 12)

Taken together, these ideas raise the importance of technology education in the classroom to the same level as science. However, it is not the same technology that was taught in decades past. Today technology education means helping students become aware of the technological world they live in, how technology and science support each other, how to learn to use new technologies as they become available, and how technological decisions we make as individuals and as a society can impact our lives and the lives of our children.

Mathematical Practices

The Common Core State Standards movement gained momentum in 2009 when the National Governor's Council and the Council of Chief State School Officers decided that it was time for the states to work together and adopt the same educational standards so that students who move from one state to another will not have to repeat the same units or miss out on key concepts and skills. The development of these standards was guided by the latest research in how students learn, effective instructional models from various states, and input from multiple organizations and the public. Most states have already adopted these Common Core State Standards in mathematics and English language arts, so that curriculum developers, teachers, and creators of assessment instruments will all be on the same page about what students should learn and how they should be assessed.

In the area of mathematics, the development of mathematical progressions presented a clear set of shared goals for what knowledge and skills students should acquire. In addition to these expectations, the Common Core State Standards for Mathematics prescribed a set of standards for "mathematical practice," which describe the varieties of expertise that educators should seek to develop in their students as they grow in their mathematical abilities and understanding. As you read through the following Standards for Mathematical Practice, notice that these practices emphasize the importance of using mathematics in everyday life in a way that connects very closely to the other STEM practices listed earlier. (The following statements are abbreviated from the *Common Core State Standards: Mathematical Practice*, 2011. The full text can be found at: www.corestandards.org/the-standards/mathematics/introduction/standards-for-mathematical-practice/.)

Practice 1: Make sense of problems and persevere with solving them. Mathematically proficient students start by explaining to themselves the meaning of a problem and looking for entry points to its solution. They check their answers and they continually ask themselves, "Does this make sense?"

Practice 2: Reason abstractly and quantitatively. Mathematically proficient students make sense of quantities and their relationships in problem situations. They know how to use and manipulate the different properties of operations and objects to solve problems.

STEM LESSON ESSENTIALS • Integrating Science, Technology, Engineering, and Mathematics

Practice 3: Construct viable arguments and critique the reasoning of others. Mathematically proficient students understand and use reasoning to analyze situations, make conjectures, and build a logical progression of statements to support their thinking. They listen or read the arguments of others, decide whether the arguments make sense, and ask useful questions to clarify or improve the arguments.

Practice 4: Model with mathematics. Mathematically proficient students can apply the mathematics they know to solve problems arising in everyday life, society, and the workplace.

Practice 5: Use appropriate tools strategically. Mathematically proficient students consider the available tools when solving a problem. They are able to use technological tools to explore and deepen their understanding of concepts.

Practice 6: Attend to precision. Mathematically proficient students try to communicate precisely to others, calculate accurately and efficiently, and express numerical answers with a degree of precision appropriate for the problem context.

Practice 7: Look for and make use of structure. Mathematically proficient students look closely to discern a pattern. They can see complicated things as single objects or as being composed of several objects to better understand how to solve more difficult problems.

Practice 8: Look for and express regularity in repeated reasoning. Mathematically proficient students notice if calculations are repetitive and look both for general methods and for shortcuts in solving more complex problems.

Connections Among the STEM Practices

The chart in Figure 5.2 lists all of the STEM practices, slightly rearranged to highlight ways in which they are similar or complementary. For example, practices in science, engineering, and mathematics all involve modeling. Both engineering and mathematics require students to define and solve problems.

Figure 5.2 Connections among the STEM practices.

Science	Engineering	Technology	Mathematics
Ask questions.	Define problems.	Become aware of the web of technological systems on which society depends.	Make sense of problems and persevere in solving them.
Develop and use models.	Develop and use models.		Model with mathematics.
Plan and carry out investigations.	Plan and carry out investigations.	Learn how to use new technologies as they become available.	Use appropriate tools strategically.
Analyze and interpret data.	Analyze and interpret data.		Attend to precision.
Use mathematics and computational thinking.	Use mathematics and computational thinking.	Recognize the role that technology plays in the advancement of science and engineering.	Reason abstractly and quantitatively.
Construct explanations.	Design solutions.		Look for and make use of structure.
Engage in argument from evidence.	Engage in argument from evidence.	Make informed decisions about technology, given its relationship to society and the environment.	Construct viable arguments and critique the reasoning of others.
Obtain, evaluate, and communicate information.	Obtain, evaluate, and communicate information.		Look for and express regularity in repeated reasoning.

Science, engineering, and mathematics require students to learn to engage in constructive argument, and technology and mathematics both call for students to learn to use technological tools appropriately, and the ability to use tools is essential for carrying out investigations and analyzing and interpreting data in science and engineering.

Concluding Thoughts

Whenever we take apart the four STEM fields, there is always the danger that they will be viewed separately, rather than integrated seamlessly. The real power

STEM LESSON ESSENTIALS • Integrating Science, Technology, Engineering, and Mathematics

in STEM teaching comes from the connections among the fields and how they support and strengthen each other, as illustrated in Figure 5.2.

This concludes an overview of the STEM practices—the capabilities that our students are expected to gain over thirteen years of schooling. It is not expected that students will learn them all in any given year, but rather as they progress from year to year, developing these "habits of thinking" as they grow in their maturity and experience.

Reflection

- After having read this chapter do you see any advantage to calling what students should be able to do in science and engineering *practices* rather than *processes*? How so?

- Which of the practices do you routinely teach? Which do you rarely teach?

- What are your thoughts about the matrix in Figure 5.2? Do you see connections by looking across the rows? Is this helpful to you in any way?

REFERENCES

Aldredge, B. G., F. Lawenz, and D. Huffman. 1997. "Scope, Sequence, and Coordination." *Science Teacher* 64 (1): 21–25.

American Association for the Advancement of Science. 1993. *Benchmarks for Science Literacy*. Project 2061. New York, London: Oxford University Press. Available at: www.project2061 .org/tools/bsl/default.htm.

Common Core State Standards Initiative. *Common Core Standards in Mathematics*. Available at: www.corestandards.org/the-standards/mathematics/.

Duschl, R. A., H. A. Schweingruber, A. W. Shouse, National Research Council (U.S.), National Research Council (U.S.)., and National Research Council (U.S.). 2007. *Taking Science to School: Learning and Teaching Science in Grades K–8*. Washington, DC: National Academies Press. Available at: www.nap.edu/catalog/11625.html.

National Research Council. 2008. *Ready, Set, Science! Putting Research to Work in K–8 Science Classrooms*. Board on Science Education, Division of Behavioral and Social Sciences and Education. Washington, DC: National Academy Press.

————. 1996. *National Science Education Standards*. Washington, DC: National Academy Press.

————. 2012. *A Framework for K–12 Science Education: Practices, Crosscutting Concepts, and Core Ideas*. Committee on New Science Education Standards, Board on Science Education, Division of Behavioral and Social Sciences and Education. Washington, DC: National Academy Press.

Pearson, G., A. T. Young, National Academy of Engineering, and National Research Council (U.S.). 2002. *Technically Speaking: Why All Americans Need to Know More About Technology*. Washington, DC: National Academy Press.

Tsupros, N., R. Kohler, and J. Hallinen. 2009. *STEM Education: A Project to Identify the Missing Components*. Pittsburgh, PA: Intermediate Unit 1 and Carnegie Mellon.

Gearing Up to Teach STEM Practices

Science, technology, engineering, and mathematics are closely interlinked areas—so closely interlinked that it is often difficult to know exactly where one starts and the other ends. Students in science classes are often taught about technology, engineering, and mathematics, while students in technology classes learn about science, engineering, and mathematics. Technologies are changing fundamentally the ways scientists work and are becoming important components of science education. Students' skills in using the tools of science are becoming components of the "new literacies."

—Technology and Engineering Literacy Framework for the 2014 National Assessment of Educational Progress, National Assessment Governing Board (2008, 1–10)

> **BEFORE READING THIS CHAPTER,** think about a teaching experience that emphasized one or more of the STEM practices. Were you the teacher or the learner? What made it memorable?

Why Gears?

Keeping in mind that *technology* refers to all of the ways that people have changed the natural world to meet human needs and achieve goals, there is an almost endless number of technologies that could serve as the foundation for a unit that teaches the STEM practices. On the pages that follow, we describe a unit designed especially for this book and tested in a number of settings with more than 100 STEM educators, with the goal of communicating what all four sets of STEM practices might look like if integrated into a single unit centered around a common technology—gears.

We chose gears for a couple of reasons. First of all, they're fun. Toy gears invite kids to fit them together in various ways and to very quickly discover the "rules" that guide their operation. Second, gears provide a means for teaching concepts in all four STEM fields. Third, toy gears are relatively inexpensive, and many teachers already have sets of gears left over from classes on simple machines. And fourth, the gears themselves offer a metaphor for how the STEM fields can function together as a coherent set of mutually reinforcing domains of knowledge and skills.

Leading with Technology

Gears are often used to teach elementary students about simple machines. After students learn about the basic forms (wedge, lever and fulcrum, wheel and axle, etc.), gears are introduced because they combine the effects of two simple machines—the wheel and axle and the lever. However, the instructional unit on simple machines has gradually disappeared from the science curriculum because it is not typically featured in standards. Nonetheless, gears can be used in a different way to illuminate the STEM practices and how they mesh with core ideas in Common State Standards. This activity is designed for students in grades 4 or 5.

It's important to use toy gears of different sizes whose teeth are divisible by a common denominator (Figure 6.1). For example, gears of eight, twelve, and sixteen teeth work nicely, as they are all divisible by four. Gear toys are generally mounted on small stems, or axles, that can be inserted into holes on a board. Some gear toys have the axles mounted on magnets so the gears can quickly be rearranged on a metal board in various configurations. Each team of three or four students will need their own set of gear toys.

Figure 6.1 It is important to use toy gears whose teeth are whole number multiples of each other. This set of gears has teeth of eight, twelve, and sixteen teeth. Notice the sticky dots that help students count rotations.

The goal of the first activity is for students to become familiar with gear technology and to build some experiences around which the other strands can later be developed. After ten or fifteen minutes of free exploration so the students get familiar with how to use the materials, the teacher gathers the students together and asks them to talk about their discoveries, recording these on the board. Depending on what the students have already found from their own initial investigations, the teacher can challenge the students to explore gears more systematically by asking questions about phenomena they might not have discovered yet, such as:

- How can you get one gear to turn another gear in the *opposite* direction?
- How can you get one gear to turn another gear in the *same* direction?

- How can you make one gear turn *two other gears*? *Three other gears*?
- How can you turn a gear *twice* and make an adjoining gear turn *once*?

Call the students together again and ask them to talk about and demonstrate what they have learned, taking care to use the phrase: "What have you learned about the technology of gears?" Notice that we use the word *technology* to refer to this toy. This is the broad use of technology to refer to "any modification of the natural world to meet a human need or achieve a goal."

A possible extension of this activity is to have the students take apart broken devices that have gears, point out different kinds of gears (bevel, spur, helical, etc.), observe that gears can be made from different materials, and note how different kinds of gears are used in different applications. If possible be prepared for this session with images of different applications of gears, such as in cars, boats, trains, and planes, in factories, in mechanical clocks, in microscopes and telescopes, in farm machinery, and in just about any machine that has spinning parts. You may want to have students conduct an Internet investigation of how and when gears evolved from earlier uses of the wheel. Encourage them to use the word *technology* when discussing gears.

To wrap up the session, ask the students to reflect on what they have learned about the technology of gears—where they are used, different kinds of gears, uses of different materials to make them, when they were invented, and so on. You could end the session by asking the students what would happen if all the gears in the world were to suddenly dissolve. What would happen? How would our lives be different?

Reflecting on Technology Practices

Consider how the above activity introduces students to technology practices, in which they are expected to become aware of the web of technological systems on which society depends, learn how to use technologies, and recognize the role that technology plays in the advancement of science and engineering.

Introducing the Science of Gears

At the heart of every technology is a natural phenomenon (Arthur 2009). The more a person knows about the phenomenon, the easier it is to improve the technology and apply it in novel ways. For example, consider the phenomenon of fire. When ancient peoples discovered how to control fire, it became a technology. Although they may not have understood it at first, they gradually became more familiar with it because it met their needs for light, to cook foods, and to scare away wild animals. Over the millennia, people learned more and more about fire until eventually they were able to use fire to launch rockets into outer space. The natural phenomenon that underlies gears involves the science of force, motion, and transfer of energy.

To introduce the science of gears, the teacher asks the students a few critical questions about ways in which the gears operate and how they can be put together to accomplish specific tasks:

- When you put two gears together and turn one, does it push the other gear or pull it? How do you know?
- How can you use gears and a piece of string to lift a paper clip?
- How do gears enable you to transfer energy from one place to another?
- What questions about gears do you have?

The purpose of these questions is to lead the students to articulate explanations for how gears function using concepts such as force, interaction, systems, and energy.

Although students may have been introduced to forces as *pushes* or *pulls* in prior years, this activity advances their understanding by asking them to think about how a force is transmitted from the tooth of one gear to the tooth of another and from a push against one gear to a pull on a string as it raises a paper clip from the floor. These ideas about forces form the conceptual building blocks needed for a deeper understanding of Newton's laws of motion that will be introduced in middle school and quantified in high school.

If the students are ready for the concept of energy transfer, the questions can be extended by asking them to think of the source of energy (themselves) or to describe how the energy is transferred from one gear to the next, into the string, and finally to a paper clip. Students can begin to define and defend their thinking based upon the evidence of the movement of the paper clip. Students should use the word science in references to fundamental knowledge about how natural and designed systems function.

Reflecting on Science Practices

Consider how the above activity introduces students to science practices, in which they are expected to ask questions, to develop and use models, plan and carry out investigations, analyze and interpret data, construct explanations, engage in argument from evidence, and obtain, evaluate, and communicate information. Although these activities are relatively simple, they nonetheless can lead to some interesting discussions in which students articulate their mental models, and use the gears as evidence to demonstrate their ideas.

Mathematics of Ratios

Ratios are challenging for students to learn. The mathematical concept of a ratio is important in building an understanding of other mathematical concepts such as fractions and trigonometric functions. The concept of a ratio is also an important precursor to many concepts in science such as speed, velocity, and density. This third set of questions introduces ratios in a simple and concrete manner. Through the following questions students should begin to recognize and apply reasoning skills to make predictions about how two gears interact.

- Find a pair of gears so that one gear will turn another gear twice. How many teeth are there on each of the two gears?
- Can you find a gear that will turn another gear three times? If such a gear exists, how many teeth would it have?

- Find a pair of gears so that if you turn one gear twice the other gear will turn three times. How many teeth are on each gear?
- What is the relationship between the number of teeth on the gear in each pair, and the number of times that each one turns? How can you represent this idea?
- If you had a gear with one hundred teeth and wanted to make a gear that would turn five times while the gear you have would turn once, how many teeth would the new gear need to have?

As the students continue to work with the toy gears, they will find that a gear that turns once and causes another gear to turn twice has twice as many teeth; a gear that turns once and causes another gear to turn three times has three times as many teeth; and so on. As students begin to express this relationship in their own words, they should be making statements comparing the number of turns to the number of gear teeth. That is the perfect teachable moment for the teacher to introduce (or perhaps remind the students about) the term *ratio*— a relationship between two numbers. The concept of equivalent fractions is perfectly expressed by comparing the ratio representing the number of teeth on two gears (for example, $^8/_{16}$) and the ratio that represents the number of turns made by the same two meshed gears (in this case, $^1/_2$).

Once they understand the mathematics of gear ratios, your students will be able to plan an entire system of gears and know how it will function when the system is assembled. Students can also investigate gear sizes, determine whether

Reflecting on Mathematics Practices

Consider how the above activity introduces students to mathematics practices, in which they are expected to make sense of problems and persevere in solving them, model with mathematics, use appropriate tools, attend to precision, reason abstractly and quantitatively, look for and make use of structure, construct viable arguments and critique the reasoning of others, and look for and express regularity.

or not gear circumference is related to the number of teeth, or see if they can use the Internet to find the smallest and largest gears ever made. Too often the word *math* is confined to use in mathematics classes, sometimes with a negative connotation. So it is important that teachers and students use the term when deciding questions such as "What is the appropriate *math* that we need to solve this problem?"

Engineering Design

In this last activity, students are presented with a problem—how to design and build a device that will display figurines to their greatest advantage, spinning gracefully side by side. The assigned task is a simple one:

> Next week is the start of the holiday shopping season, and your boss would like you to create a window display that will capture the attention of shoppers. She hands you several figurines of angels and a box of toy gears and she says she wants you to create an eye-catching moving display. When you ask her to say more about what she wants you to do, she just says, "Use your imagination! Just make it great!"[1]

The students now have the conceptual and physical tools they need to solve the problem. They know they can use the toy gears to build a moving display. However, the problem is somewhat vague. Should they display just one figurine, or several? Should the figurines spin at the same rate, or is it better for one to spin faster than the others? Should they all spin in the same direction or in different directions? Should it be obvious the figurines are attached to the gears or should they make it look more "magical"?

At this point in the unit, the students know enough about gears to plan a display in any way that they choose, and any choice they make would be an acceptable solution. That is one of the hallmarks of the engineering aspect of the STEM lesson—that there are many different or possible solutions.

---

[1]Inspired by Children's Engineering Educators, LLC. *Gears 1, 2, and 3*. Posted online at: www.galaxy .net/~k12/machines/.

STEM LESSON ESSENTIALS • Integrating Science, Technology, Engineering, and Mathematics

You can require that team members sketch their display and predict how the figurines will move before you give them the materials to build it. That will help them put what they learned into practice—by creating an engineering plan—which they will then test and modify if they wish, by actually building their display.

Different groups of students would very likely create different displays, so that after the students complete their displays the class could participate in a discussion of which would be the best. The teacher could inject some rigor to the process of evaluation by asking the class to discuss and agree on what makes a good window display and then to rate each of the designs based on those characteristics (criteria). Ideally team members should have a chance to redesign their window displays and finally articulate how their design best meets the criteria for a successful solution.

Wrap up by asking the students to reflect on how they applied what they learned about technology, science, and mathematics to solve this engineering problem. Point out that professional engineers are often called upon to improve a technology or use a technology—gears in this case—to solve a problem, or

Reflecting on Engineering Practices

Referring to the chart in the previous chapter (Figure 5.1), engineering practices include: define problems, develop and use models, plan and carry out investigations, analyze and interpret data, use mathematics and computational thinking, design solutions, engage in argument from evidence, and obtain, evaluate, and communicate information. Notice that engineering practices are similar to but also somewhat different from science practices. In contrast to science, which starts with a question, engineering starts with a problem to solve. Consequently, similar practices serve different goals. For example, science models and simulations are usually used to represent some aspect of the natural world; in engineering, models and simulations are generally used to test designs to see how well they solve the problem. There is also a difference in the end product. Science involves explaining a phenomenon, while engineering involves producing and communicating a final design.

design something that will work in a desired way. That's why engineers study mathematics and science—so they can understand the science behind the technology and use mathematics to solve the problem in the best way possible. Encourage your students to use the terms *engineer* and *engineering* in situations where it is necessary to think creatively to solve a problem to meet people's needs or achieve a goal.

Concluding Thoughts

Reflection is one of the four essential strands identified in *Ready, Set, Science!* (Michaels et al. 2008), a report from the National Research Council that summarizes research in science education. That is, it is important for students to reflect on the nature of science and on their own learning process. Engaging students in reflecting on the different activities of the unit can provide them with an understanding of how the four STEM fields fit together.

It will be important for the teacher to point out that although these four capabilities are distinct, people move fluidly from one to the other when working on real problems. When working with gears, for example, it was not necessary to stop before counting gear teeth and say, "Okay, now I'll do some math." The STEM strands work together as a whole, just as four gears mesh smoothly and work together to accomplish a task (Figure 6.2). While it is valuable to

Reflection

- Reflecting on the curriculum you currently teach, which STEM practices do you routinely present to your students?

- Do you sometimes shift gears in the same unit to illustrate the connections between two ideas, disciplines, or skills?

- For a unit that you expect to teach in the future, can you think of a new twist that would enable you to introduce a new STEM practice?

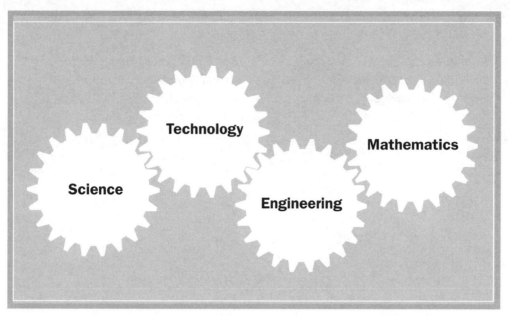

Figure 6.2 The STEM strands work together as a whole, just as four gears mesh smoothly and work together to accomplish a task.

reflect on the four fields separately from time to time, it is even more important to see how they function as a whole.

REFERENCES

Arthur, W. B. 2009. *The Nature of Technology: What It Is and How It Evolves*. New York: Free Press.

Bybee, R. W., et al. 1989. *Science and Technology Education for the Elementary Years: Frameworks for Curriculum and Instruction*. Washington, DC: The National Center for Improving Instruction.

CCSSO and NGA. 2010. *Common Core State Standards for Mathematics. Common Core Standards Initiative*. Washington, DC: Council of Chief State School Officers (CCSSO) and National Governor's Association. Available at: www.corestandards.org.

ITEEA. 2007. *Standards for Technological Literacy: Content for the Study of Technology*. International Technology and Engineering Education Association. Reston, VA: ITEEA. Available at: www.iteea.org/TAA/PDFs/Execsum.pdf.

Michaels, S., A. W. Shouse, and H. A. Schweingruber. 2008. *Ready, Set, Science! Putting Research to Work in K–8 Science Classrooms*. Board on Science Education, Center for Education,

Division of Behavioral and Social Sciences and Education. Washington, DC: The National Academies Press. Available at: www.nap.edu/catalog.php?record_id=11882.

National Assessment Governing Board (NAGB). 2008. *Technology and Engineering Literacy Framework for the 2014 National Assessment of Educational Progress* (NAEP). Available at: http://www.nagb.org/publications/frameworks/prepub_naep_tel_framework_2014.pdf.

CHAPTER 7

Why Technology and Engineering?

Engineering and technology are featured alongside the physical sciences, life sciences, and earth and space sciences for two critical reasons: to reflect the importance of understanding the human-built world and to recognize the value of better integrating the teaching and learning of science, engineering, and technology.

—*A Framework for K–12 Science Education: Practices, Crosscutting Concepts, and Core Ideas*, National Research Council (2012, 8)

BEFORE READING THIS CHAPTER, make a list of the pros and cons for introducing engineering and technology into the science and mathematics curriculum.

Children Are Natural Engineers

Children are quick to answer the question, "Why technology and engineering?" by their enthusiasm for creative design and problem-solving activities. Introducing technology and engineering into the classroom is not unlike taking children to the beach or the sandbox and helping them build sand castles. Bring along a few tools, such as toy shovels and pails, to help the children realize their vision; and as they build they will come to better understand the properties of the tools and materials they are working with. Too much water and the castle wall melts. Too little and it crumbles. On subsequent trips the children will continue to learn and their sand castles will grow in complexity, along with their knowledge and skills. That is, fun and engaging activities combined with tools and materials gradually mature into knowledge and skills.

The parallel between building sand castles and including technology and engineering education in the classroom makes even more sense when we consider the different kinds of technologies that children need to learn about to understand the world in which they live. Keeping in mind that technologies are the ways that people modify the world to meet human needs and reach goals, a few major technologies come to mind, along with the kinds of knowledge and abilities that children need to acquire through the K–12 years. For each of these technologies, think of ways that your students could engage with them in ways that are fun, while enriching their understanding and skills.

Transportation. Why are cars, boats, and planes needed? How do they work? What problems do they create? How can they be improved to serve people's needs while causing fewer problems?

Construction. What kinds of structures do people build? What properties do they need to have to meet people's needs? What tools and materials are used to build them? How are these structures organized into cities and towns, connected by networks of highways and rails? What are some of the problems that develop with continued growth and expansion? How can these problems be solved?

Electricity. What are the ways we use electricity every day? How would our lives be different if our electricity were suddenly cut off? How is electricity generated? Where does our electricity come from? What are some of the problems associated with increasing demands for more electricity? What are ways to reduce our need for electricity or to generate electricity in ways that avoid some of these problems?

Medicine. What are the different medical products and procedures we know about? Why are they important? What might happen if we no longer had access to them? What are the limits of today's medical practices? Are medical services available to everyone around the world? What are some of the medical problems that need to be solved?

Food and water. Fresh, clean water is mainly responsible for increasing life expectancy in the United States from about forty years in 1900 to more than seventy-five years in 2000. And methods of agriculture have greatly improved crop yields so as to feed the world's billions. Nonetheless, there continues to be lack of clean water and famine in parts of the world. As the world's population grows ever more rapidly, increasing from six billion just twelve years ago to seven billion in 2011, there will be an even greater need for improved water purification and agricultural technologies.

Communication. Computers and related digital technologies, from satellites to cell phones, have transformed communications over the past fifty years, knitting together people around the world. Why have these different forms of communication grown so rapidly? What are the different ways they are used by people in different professions? How do digital communications devices work? Which are dependent on new developments in hardware, and which on new ways to use the hardware? What changes might we expect in the future?

At the heart of each of these technologies lie scientific concepts and principles that students need to learn to better understand the technologies and engineer solutions to problems. By presenting the science in the context of technological explorations, such as the gear activities presented in Chapter 6, students will learn the concepts and how to apply them at the same time. Learning science will be contextualized and consequently more meaningful.

Similarly, well-designed and sequenced classroom activities with technologies as the focus will lead to a need for mathematical concepts and principles. Working with gears naturally leads to a need to understand gear ratios. Building structures requires knowledge of measuring, scaling, and measuring area and volume. Constructing electrical circuits involves reading analog and digital meters and creating diagrams of circuits using symbols.

Combining learning in the four STEM fields leads to better understanding of concepts and improvement in skills because these four fields support each other. The totality engages students' interest and imbues their activities with meaning and relevance.

A New Role for Education

In the history of our species, education has been the means for transmitting the most important cultural beliefs, knowledge, and abilities of a society from one generation to the next. Long before there were schools, children learned from their elders. They practiced the skills that they would need as adults through play, and the fundamental ideas and ways of thinking were shared through stories.

Given the rate at which human society is changing, it is not surprising that our educational system must change to keep pace. As recently as fifty years ago, it was sufficient for people to be able to read, write, and do simple arithmetic to hold most jobs and function as consumers and citizens. Today's children must graduate from an educational system that prepares them to understand the world of the twenty-first century, where they will be expected to work with technologies that were not invented when they were students, to make informed decisions about major engineering projects as citizens and voters, and to solve problems in their everyday lives that could not have been anticipated by their teachers.

We are now part of the global community and our lives are more complex; therefore it is more important than ever that students have the opportunity to not only become better prepared for postsecondary careers but also become citizens of this global community who can analyze situations, think critically, and problem solve. Some of today's children will choose to pursue careers in STEM fields, where they will be responsible for solving critical problems, such as the need for safe and nonpolluting sources of electrical energy, how to grow sufficient food for the world's billions, what to do about rising sea levels, and how to solve problems that we cannot even anticipate today. Students who choose not to enter STEM fields will be called upon to make decisions about technological issues as voters and consumers and to solve problems in their own lives. Consequently *all students* must become literate in the STEM fields.

Concluding Thoughts

STEM capabilities work together as a whole, just as four gears mesh smoothly and work together to accomplish a task. Although not all activities can or should involve all four STEM fields, opportunities to reflect from time to time on which of the STEM fields was involved will help students develop a sense of the kinds of knowledge and skills that are needed in a new situation, to solve a problem that they encounter, or to meet a goal.

Combining science and math with technology and engineering—integrated STEM learning—not only has great promise to enable students to learn concepts and skills more rapidly and more deeply, but will provide both the motivation and the disposition to apply what students learn to issues that they find relevant and important.

Reflection

- Consider the list of pros and cons that you listed at the beginning of this chapter. Did any of the ideas in this chapter help you think further about these ideas? Do you want to edit your original list?

- One of the objections to integrating technology and engineering into the science curriculum is that it leaves less time for science, which some people contend is a more fundamental field of endeavor. Do you agree with this position? Why or why not?

REFERENCE

National Research Council. 2012. *A Framework for K–12 Science Education: Practices, Crosscutting Concepts, and Core Ideas.* Committee on New Science Education Standards, Board on Science Education, Division of Behavioral and Social Sciences and Education. Washington, DC: National Academy Press. Available at: www.nap.edu/catalog.php?record_id=13165.

CHAPTER 8

Three Approaches to Integrated STEM

BEFORE YOU READ THIS CHAPTER, think about how you would characterize the kind of STEM integration of the Gears unit in Chapter 6. What in the unit enabled the students to see how the four STEM fields were joined together?

STEM education is an interdisciplinary approach to learning which removes the traditional barriers separating the four disciplines of science, technology, engineering, and mathematics, and integrates them into meaningful experiences for students.

—*Making STEM Real*, Hoachlander and Yanofsky (2011)

What Does *Integration* Mean?

When you ask fourth graders about their day at school, most will respond with something like the following: "We did reading in the morning, then we had our reading groups, then we had recess and math before lunch." Students view these subjects as entirely separate because they are typically based on different standards and taught with curriculum materials that were developed without reference to each other. One of the great promises of STEM is in breaking down the isolation of science and mathematics—from each other and from the fabric of technology and design in the world outside of school. The idea of STEM teaching and learning is to increase student engagement, to deepen their understanding, to raise achievement, and to help them see the relevance in what they are learning (Hoachlander and Yanofsky 2011).

STEM education represents a fundamentally different approach to organizing the school curriculum. As such, it raises a number of practical questions. What does *integration* really mean? Is it sufficient for students to see the connections between concepts in different fields? Or does it mean assimilating concepts from two different fields so they become one? Should integration involve skills as well as concepts? How about connections to social studies? Language arts? Or to everyday life? These are important questions that we will address in this chapter.

Three Approaches

In the book *Meeting Standards Through Integrated Curriculum*, Drake and Burns (2004) begin by acknowledging that integrating the curricular areas is not a new idea, and reference a 1935 publication from the National Council of Teachers of English, which offered a range of definitions, from "casual attention to related materials in other subjects" to "the unification of all subjects and experiences." Drake and Burns further develop these ideas as three approaches to integration. Following is our own slightly modified scheme that we feel is especially suitable to describing different levels of STEM integration. In brief, they are: *multidisciplinary or thematic integration*, *interdisciplinary integration*, and *transdisciplinary integration*.

In the remainder of this chapter, we will illustrate how each of the approaches might be used to teach students about our solar system. Before we do that, however, we would like to emphasize three important points:

First, integration does not mean abandoning standards. It is still important that our students acquire all of the concepts and skills identified in standards documents; these are generally described within disciplinary areas.

Second, the real power of STEM lies in the integration of the subject areas so that students begin to see how the concepts and skills from different disciplines can work together to help them answer intriguing questions and solve meaningful problems.

Third, an integrated STEM curriculum shifts the teacher's focus from how to teach the concepts and skills within each discipline to how to help their students learn *to apply* STEM concepts and skills and relate what they are learning to the rest of their school day.

Multidisciplinary or Thematic Integration

The multidisciplinary, or thematic, approach connects the individual disciplines by organizing the curriculum around a common theme such as "Oceans," "Ecosystems," "Flight," or "Pirates." This approach is used to provide coherence to the curriculum so that the students have an opportunity to see that they can learn about something in many different ways. For example, a theme of "Pirates" might initially be suggested by an English teacher who is having her students read *Treasure Island* by Robert Lewis Stevenson. The science teacher might then have students learn about ships with a unit on buoyancy, and the social studies teacher assigns a chapter from a textbook on the real history of pirates. In math class students could learn what a gold doubloon would be worth in today's currency, and so on.

Although this multidisciplinary or thematic integrated approach has the advantage of helping students connect ideas across domains and apply skills in an engaging context, it runs the risk of becoming an uncoordinated "potpourri" of subjects. By analogy, think of the junk drawer in your kitchen. It contains miscellaneous items that are put together for convenience but which you probably do not use as often as your drawer for the silverware, which also contains different items, but where items are organized by closely related functions.

For the multidisciplinary approach to serve as a rich, relevant, and effective educational tool, it is important for the multidisciplinary theme to capture students' interests and to enable students to meet the educational standards associated with each discipline.

Example of a Multidisciplinary Approach

Imagine a teachers' meeting in which they have just decided to organize a grade-level thematic unit on the solar system.

Science Teacher: "The new science textbook does a nice job of describing what we know today about the solar system, but I'd like to get the kids more involved in learning the features of the different planets, such as the rings of Saturn and Jupiter's Great Red Spot, and how the planets move around the Sun."

PE Teacher: "I could have the students play the part of planets on the activity field. I would stand in the middle to be the Sun and have the kids playing the part of inner planets run in circles around me. It would be a good test to see if they remember from science class how fast the different planets are supposed to move."

Art Teacher: "I could have the students make models of the planets using colored clay and then make mobiles so the kids could take them home and hang them up."

Math Teacher: "I could have the students practice dividing by big numbers to see how the distance to the Moon compares to the distance to the Sun, planets, and stars."

English Teacher: "I can change my schedule so the students read a science fiction book at about the same time. In the story the students invent an antigravity paint, which they use to build a spaceship and fly to Mars."

Social Studies Teacher: "I plan to teach a unit on mythology. That would provide a good opportunity for the students to learn about the origin of the names of the planets and their association with Greek and Roman gods and goddesses."

As illustrated in this imaginary scenario, multidisciplinary integration has advantages over business as usual. Students experience a more coherent series of lessons and activities, requiring only small changes by their teachers, such as modifying their schedules, finding relevant media, or changing worksheets to reflect the common theme. This thematic curriculum plan for a unit on the solar system is illustrated in Figure 8.1.

Figure 8.1 illustrates that all of the activities are somehow connected to the solar system. However, the connections tend to be peripheral—they are related but do not focus on a common understanding among the teachers of the most important key concepts or essential skills that would help their students develop a deeper understanding of the solar system. Also, there are no obvious connections between the different disciplines, other than their common connection to the solar system.

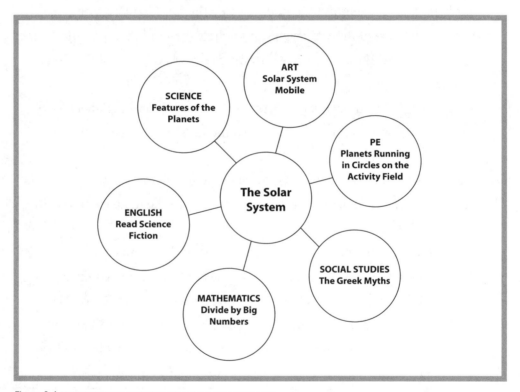

Figure 8.1 Multidisciplinary curriculum plan about the solar system.

Interdisciplinary Integration

In this approach to integration, teachers organize the curriculum around common learning across disciplines. They chunk together the common learning embedded in the disciplines to emphasize interdisciplinary skills and concepts. The disciplines are identifiable, but they assume less importance than in the multidisciplinary approach. Therefore, the first step in designing this type of STEM curriculum is to choose a key concept or skill that is important for all students to learn and that is enriched by combining knowledge and skills from two or more disciplines.

Interdisciplinary integration should not be viewed as entirely distinct from thematic or multidisciplinary integration. Both approaches aim at providing a curriculum that is coherent from the viewpoint of the learner. Also, interdisciplinary integration can occur within a thematic curriculum plan, whenever the theme includes an important key concept that is taught from the viewpoint of two or more disciplines.

Interdisciplinary integration can also link entirely different disciplines, such as science and mathematics, or technology and social studies. In the multidisciplinary approach, the focus is on one main topic as in the example in Figure 8.1; in the case of the interdisciplinary approach, learning goals from two disciplines are "fused" to form a single key concept or skill—just as a chain consists of individual links but functions as a whole.

Although taking this interdisciplinary approach further may at first sound daunting, an example or two will illustrate that it is not all that difficult to accomplish.

Example of an Interdisciplinary Approach

Suppose the science teacher from the multidisciplinary example begins with a different question—one that requires teaching a concept that is shared with a different discipline. What might that conversation look like?

Science Teacher: "The new science textbook does a nice job of describing what we know today about the solar system, but I'd like my kids to have a better concept of scale—like the huge range of sizes of the planets and how far apart they are in space. Can anyone help me with that?"

Mathematics Teacher: "If you mean understanding the scale of the solar system, I heard about an activity in which students use the same scale for the size of the planets as for the distance they are from the Sun. It's called 'The Earth as a Peppercorn' (Ottewell 1989) and it shows you just how much space there is in space! I've been having the students work on ratios, and I'd like to have the students figure out the sizes and distances in their model if I give them the scale factor."

In this approach, the teachers organize the curriculum around common learnings across the disciplines. They chunk together the common learnings embedded in the disciplines to emphasize the interdisciplinary skills and concepts. Remember, the disciplines are still identifiable, but they assume less importance than in the multidisciplinary approach. And in this case the key concept of scale helps the students understand the solar system at a much deeper level than would be possible from learning about surface features of the planets alone, while providing good practice in applying their abilities to use ratios. This conceptually integrated curriculum plan of the two disciplines is illustrated in Figure 8.2.

In the integrated plan, the link between science and mathematics is at a deep conceptual level. From the mathematics teachers' perspective, students are

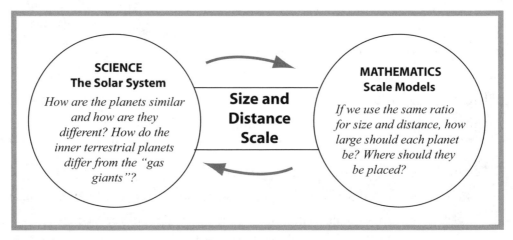

Figure 8.2 Interdisciplinary curriculum plan about the solar system.

STEM LESSON ESSENTIALS • Integrating Science, Technology, Engineering, and Mathematics

using their growing understanding of ratios to figure out how to properly scale a model, given data about the real sizes and distances in the solar system. From the science teachers' perspective, actually creating the model helps the students grasp the vast size and distance differences in the solar system better than any textbook illustration could provide. It also helps the students discover—from their modeling experience—that there are two broad categories of planets: the small terrestrial planets, including Earth, that are close to the Sun, and the four huge gas giant planets, including Jupiter, Saturn, Uranus, and Neptune. If Pluto is added to the model, students can also see how different it is from any of the major planets, being much further from the Sun than the terrestrial planets and much smaller than the gas giants.

Interdisciplinary Integration of More Than Two Disciplines

The interdisciplinary curriculum plan about the solar system described here is a good starting point for a more comprehensive curriculum. To see how such a plan can be expanded to include more disciplines, imagine how the faculty meeting described previously might proceed after the mathematics and science teachers agree to work together.

Science Teacher: "I was wondering if I might also get some help from social studies since I know that you are teaching about world history during the sixteenth and seventeenth centuries. The textbook we are using in science tells the story of how Galileo's use of the telescope helped people realize that Copernicus was right—that the Earth circles the Sun like the other planets. But it would be better if they could learn more about why this was such a controversial idea at the time."

Social Studies Teacher: "Actually, I can do better than that. I am teaching a unit about people who have been persecuted for their ideas. One of the people that our students will learn about was Giordano Bruno, who was burned at the stake in the year 1600 for expressing the idea that the Sun is a star and that there is an infinite number of habitable planets in space. That was just ten years before Galileo published his famous book, *The Sidereal Messenger*, about his observations of the Moon and Jupiter."

Science Teacher: "Thank you, that's perfect! Galileo's use of the telescope to show that the Moon had mountains and valleys like Earth, and that Jupiter had its own moons, changed people's understanding of the solar system forever. It would certainly be great if the kids could look through a telescope themselves and see what Galileo saw."

Career and Technical Education (CTE) Teacher: "I can help with that. We can buy some inexpensive kits with the materials for making small telescopes like Galileo's. Since each kit includes just two lenses and a sliding tube, it's hard to hold it steady to get a good look at the Moon or Jupiter. But making mountings for the telescope will be a great engineering project for the kids. I have some scrap wood, and I can show them pictures of different kinds of telescope mountings to get them started."

Mathematics Teacher: "And I can help the students calculate the magnifying power of their telescopes. Magnifying power is just the ratio of the focal lengths of the two lenses. I can have the students measure the focal length of the two lenses by turning off the lights and holding each lens near the wall to focus a picture of things outdoors. The distance between the lens and the wall when the picture is sharp and clear is the focal length. It's another good application of ratios."

This interdisciplinary unit is illustrated in Figure 8.3.

On the right side of Figure 8.3, between the science and mathematics circles, is a key concept about the sizes and distances of solar system bodies. That concept enriches the students' understanding of the solar system as it meets the educational goals of both the science and mathematics teachers.

At the top of the diagram is the key concept of how technology has increased our understanding of the solar system. This key concept helps students under-

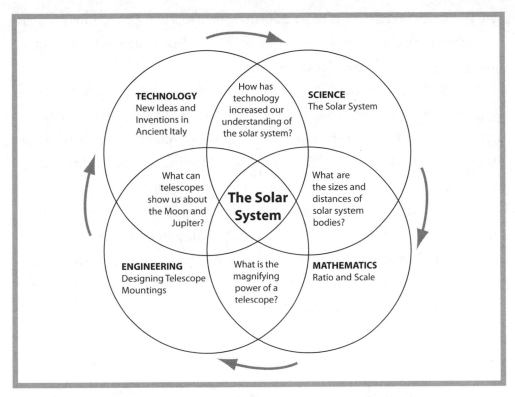

Figure 8.3 Interdisciplinary curriculum plan about the solar system.

stand where our knowledge of the solar system comes from. It also meets the science teachers' goal of helping students understand the role of technological inventions in advancing scientific understanding and the social studies teachers' goal of helping students understand how new ideas are introduced into society, sometimes at great peril to independent thinkers.

The left side of the diagram identifies what telescopes reveal about the Moon and Jupiter as a key concept. Galileo's observations that the Moon looked like an actual place, somewhat like the Earth, and was not a perfect sphere were very important in helping people think of the planets as worlds. Likewise his observations of Jupiter showed that it was like a mini–solar system, with four tiny moons going around it, suggesting that Copernicus was right and that Earth is not the center of the universe, but it circles the Sun along with the other planets. This part of the plan would not be nearly as rich without the help of the CTE teacher, whose skills helping students design and build simple structures helped students see the Moon and Jupiter as Galileo did, but with slightly improved optics and a steadier mounting.

The unit does not have to stop there. The English teacher could have students read excerpts from Galileo's original text, including the passage and drawing that Galileo published soon after he saw the Moon through a telescope for the first time (Figure 8.4). The students could then write about their own observations and impressions and make their own drawings.

It is important to point out that interdisciplinary STEM teaching does not have to be accomplished by a team of teachers. Although teamwork has the advantage of bringing together teachers with complementary expertise and helps students see the subject from different points of view, a single teacher can accomplish conceptual integration by intentionally bringing together the

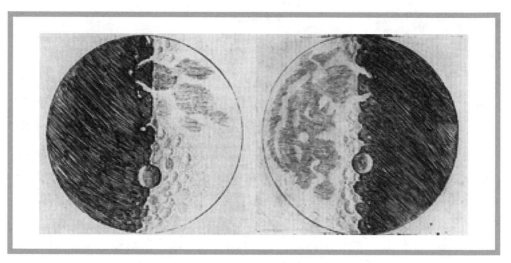

"From these observations I have been led to the opinion and conviction that the surface of the moon is not smooth, uniform, and precisely spherical as a great number of philosophers believe it (and the other heavenly bodies) to be, but is uneven, rough, and full of cavities and prominences, being not unlike the face of the earth, relieved by chains of mountains and deep valleys."

(Drake 1957, 31–35, translation of The Starry Messenger by Galileo Galilei, 1610)

Figure 8.4 The first telescopic observations of the Moon.

learning objectives of two different disciplines with a focus on a single key concept.

Transdisciplinary Integration

In the transdisciplinary approach to integration, teachers organize curriculum around student questions and concerns. This is where we ask students to take ownership of the learning and apply their knowledge and skills in a real-world context. In the transdisciplinary approach, the relevance of the students' learning and their ability to use their knowledge in a real-world application becomes the focal point. The essential question is the driver, the STEM learning objectives are the road map, and the students' previous experiences are the guideposts.

The transdisciplinary approach is grounded in constructivist theory (Fortus et al. 2005), which has been shown to improve student achievement in higher-level cognitive tasks, such as scientific processes and mathematical problem solving (Satchwell and Loepp 2002).

In the transdisciplinary approach, teachers bring together the twenty-first-century skills, knowledge, and attitudes with real-world application and problem-solving strategies. Layering on real-world, problem/project-based strategies provides a deeper and more relevant learning experience. These real-world problems are not well defined and do not have only one right answer.

Example of the Transdisciplinary Approach

To envision how a transdisciplinary unit might be developed about the solar system, let's go back to the grade-level teacher meeting and imagine the conversation that could lead to a transdisciplinary experience for students.

> **Science Teacher:** "The students have enjoyed the solar system unit, especially the chance to build a telescope and look through it to see Jupiter and its moons. But they still aren't as involved as I'd like them to be. I wish

I could put them in a rocket ship and fly them to the planets so they could really see what it is like to be there and have to deal with life on an alien world."

Art Teacher: "How about asking them to imagine being a weather reporter on another world? Maybe they could see what the weather is like on the other planets and give updates for local, national, and international weather for Mars or Saturn."

Science Teacher: "That's a great idea! They could work in groups, and each group could be assigned to give a weather report from a different planet. But first they would need to find out how people on Earth create weather forecasts. I guess the driving question would be: 'How would a meteorologist forecast the weather on Planet X?' That will get them thinking about how people predict the weather here on Earth and to imagine what it would be like to survive on another planet."

Career and Technical Education (CTE) Teacher: "It would also help the students find out about a lot of different careers—meteorologists and all sorts of jobs in the television industry. Perhaps I can contact some guest speakers from the university, the weather service, and even the local TV stations. Maybe we can take them on a tour of a TV studio, where they can find out about how many different kinds of jobs are needed to produce a television show."

Mathematics Teacher: "They're going to need some math if they want to send weather reports from another world. What if someone in the studio asks them a question? How much time will it take for the radio transmission to reach them and for them to send back an answer? That could be a challenge because the distances between the planets are always changing, but I know of a computer model of the solar system that the kids could use to figure that out for different dates and times. It would be a great introduction to mathematical modeling."

Art Teacher: "I could have the kids make studio sets for their weather forecasts. They could figure out what they'd need to do to make their sets as authentic as possible."

English Teacher: "I can help the students write their scripts. I'd start by contacting the local TV station so they could see what a real TV script looks like for the weather reporter. Technical writing is another career they might not have thought of."

Science Teacher: "Thanks, everyone! This will really get the kids engaged. I've always wanted my students to think of the planets as real worlds—just as Galileo did when he first looked at the Moon through a telescope and saw mountains and valleys. By working together we can also help them learn about the real world of weather prediction and television careers right here on Earth."

Equally important as the planning that goes into a transdisciplinary unit is the practice of listening to the students' ideas and allowing them to collaborate in deciding what comes next. This approach, in which the teacher sets the goal and invites the students to help figure out how to achieve it, is well supported by research (Drake and Burns 2004). In this case, the goal was embedded in the essential question: "How would a meteorologist forecast the weather on Planet X?" Each teacher stated the goal a little differently, so as to help the students acquire concepts and skills in their discipline, but in each case the students had some freedom to lead the exploration and express their own creative ideas. The structure of the unit is illustrated in Figure 8.5.

Figure 8.5 illustrates the essential question that drives the unit as a whole and each of the discipline-based learning objectives. The enduring understandings are those ideas that you want the students to recall five or even ten years after the unit. From the students' point of view, the focus is on the project they are completing. From the teachers' point of view, the focus is on embedding

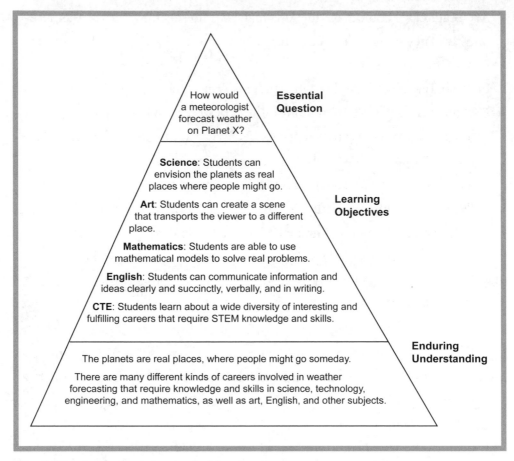

Figure 8.5 Transdisciplinary curriculum plan about the solar system.

the learning objectives so that students gain concepts and skills as they complete the project. The boundaries between the disciplines dissolve as students become more deeply immersed in the project.

Bear in mind that for the students to successfully complete a project of this type, it is necessary for them to have gained some level of knowledge and skill in the different disciplines first, probably in a more traditional learning context. Therefore, this type of integration is not something that is done every week or month and may be something that you organize and have the students do every quarter as a culmination of the learning that has been taking place.

STEM LESSON ESSENTIALS • Integrating Science, Technology, Engineering, and Mathematics

Summary of the Three STEM Approaches

The three approaches introduced in this chapter can be used at any level of education, from elementary through graduate school. They can be planned and presented by a team of teachers or by a single teacher. And they can be enriched further by integrating authentic assessment tasks and by applying the principles of backward design (Wiggins and McTighe 2004). As illustrated in Figure 8.6, the approaches are not distinct, but rather fall along a continuum from less integrated to more integrated.

All of these ways of organizing the curriculum have value. None of these approaches are "wrong," and the difference among them is the matter of degree, rather than a difference in kind. And although integrated STEM teaching is recommended by the authors of this book, it is by no means the only way to teach.

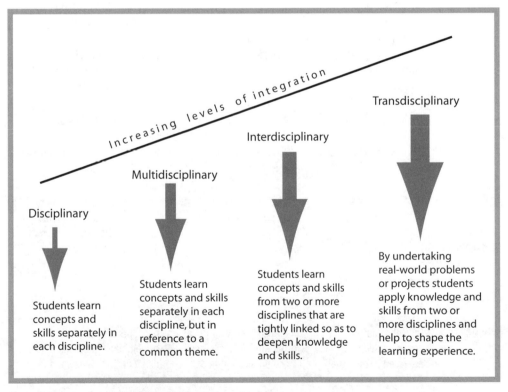

Figure 8.6 A continuum of STEM approaches to curriculum integration.

In fact, a mixture of methods is probably best. Additional differences among the three integrated approaches are shown in Figure 8.7.

Figure 8.7 Three approaches to designing integrated STEM curriculum units.

	Multidisciplinary	Interdisciplinary	Transdisciplinary
Organizing Center	Standards of the disciplines are organized around a theme.	Interdisciplinary skills and concepts are embedded in the disciplinary standards.	Problem/project based, in a real-life context, with student-driven questions.
Development of the Content	Knowledge and skills are best learned through the structure of each discipline.	Knowledge and skills are interconnected and interdependent.	Knowledge and skills are partly determined by the teacher and partly by the students.
Role of the Disciplines	Distinct skills and concepts of disciplines are taught independent of the other disciplines. Procedures of disciplines are considered most important.	Interdisciplinary skill, practices, and concepts are woven throughout. Procedures combine qualities of different disciplines.	Discipline boundaries are de-emphasized as students work on a real-life problem or project. Procedures are at least partially determined by the students in response to goals set by the teacher.
Role of Teacher	Lead instruction and facilitate student learning in each discipline.	Lead instruction and facilitate student learning across disciplines.	Set goals, facilitate student learning across disciplines, and invite students to help shape the learning experience.
Learning Goals	Discipline-specific concepts and skills.	Concepts and skills that bridge between the disciplines.	Concepts and skills that bridge between the disciplines, real-world contexts, and students' interests and concerns.
Degree of Integration	Low	Moderate	Extensive
Assessment	Discipline-based concepts and skills assessed in the usual/ customary way.	Interdisciplinary concepts and skills assessed by combining methods from different disciplines.	Concepts and skills assessed by combining methods from different disciplines, and involving students in evaluating their own work.

STEM LESSON ESSENTIALS • Integrating Science, Technology, Engineering, and Mathematics

Concluding Thoughts

Before concluding this chapter, we would like to raise the question of how explicit teachers should be when using these integrative approaches. It is common for teachers who are using a thematic approach to explain the theme to students, parents, and the entire school community. Some faculties call attention to a theme not only in academic classes, but also with art displays in the hallways, plays and concerts, and even menus for school lunches. However, it is less common that teachers call attention to interdisciplinary integration, perhaps because the concepts are so closely entwined.

In our view it is valuable for the students to know whenever disciplines are being combined—such as understanding the value of mathematics in science or of technology in history—because it helps students see how what they learn in different domains applies to key concepts. If students are to eventually see these connections for themselves, it is important for them to experience an integrated curriculum before they reach high school, where courses in the different disciplines are separated by such barriers as course names and credits.

We have for so long been focused on a silo approach to meet the standards and pass the test that moving along this continuum may take considerable effort. However, as you read the next few chapters, we believe you will become more experienced with designing STEM curricula. You will also gain ideas for making in-depth connections among the disciplines and hopefully begin to think about how you can begin this STEM integration journey.

Reflection

- Recall the three approaches to integrated STEM. Have you done any of these in your own teaching? If so, which approaches have you used?

- Which of the three approaches do you think would be most helpful for a specific purpose in your curriculum? (Keep in mind that all three approaches are helpful, but in different contexts or for different purposes.)

REFERENCES

Curtis, D. 2002. "The Power of Projects." *Educational Leadership* 60 (1): 50–53.

Drake, S. 1957. *Discoveries and Opinions of Galileo*. Garden City, NY: Doubleday Anchor Books. Translation and Notes on *The Starry Messenger* by Galileo Galilei, published by Thomas Baglioni in Venice Italy in 1610.

Drake, S. M., and R. C. Burns. 2004. *Meeting Standards Through Integrated Curriculum*. Alexandria, VA: Association for Supervision and Curriculum Development.

Fortus, D., J. Krajcik, R. C. Dershimerb, R. W. Marx, and R. Mamlok-Naamand. 2005. "Design-Based Science and Real-World Problem Solving." *International Journal of Science Education* 27 (7): 855–79.

Hoachlander, G., and D. Yanofsky. 2011. "Making STEM Real: *ASCD Educational Leadership* (March). Available at: http://naf.org/in-the-news/making-stem-real-ed-leadership.

Ottewell, G. 1989. The Thousand Yard Model, or The Earth as a Peppercorn. Raynham, MA: National Optical Astronomy Observatory.

Satchwell, R., and F. L. Loepp. 2002. "Designing and Implementing Integrated Mathematics, Science, and Technology Curriculum for the Middle School." *Journal of Industrial Teacher Education* (Spring).

Wiggins, G. and J. McTighe. 2004. Understanding by Design Professional Development Workshop. Alexandria, VA: Association for Supervision and Curriculum Development (ASCD).

Cootie Bugs Unite Science and Mathematics

Practice 3: Construct Viable Arguments and Critique the Reasoning of Others: Mathematically proficient students are also able to compare the effectiveness of two plausible arguments, distinguish correct logic or reasoning from that which is flawed, and—if there is a flaw in an argument—explain what it is. Elementary students can construct arguments using concrete referents such as objects, drawings, diagrams, and actions. Such arguments can make sense and be correct, even though they are not generalized or made formal until later grades.

—Common Core Standards in Mathematics.
Online at http://www.corestandards.org/the-standards/mathematics/

BEFORE YOU READ THIS CHAPTER, reflect on any ways that you have used an interdisciplinary approach to integrate your mathematics and science lessons. Keep in mind that mathematics does not always involve numbers— mathematical ideas can also involve logical thinking.

Meet the Cootie Bugs

Have you ever seen a "cootie bug"? Probably not, because they are a small, wingless insect, also known as a *louse*, which can get on the skin and hair of mammals. Hopefully you have never seen the real bug, but you may have heard students on the playground calling out that so-and-so has cooties or seen them running up to someone to tag and give them the imaginary cooties.

For the following activities, we are going to have some fun with our imaginary cootie bugs using developmentally appropriate science and mathematics for third through fifth grades. These activities will serve as an introduction to the idea that organisms must be adapted to their habitat or they may not survive. They will show that certain characteristics, or traits, enable organisms to survive in their habitat. For example, an organism's color may provide camouflage so predators do not see it or it may have long limbs that enable it to run fast and catch prey. Having a color that matches the surroundings and long limbs are traits that help organisms survive in their habitats.

In addition to this life science core idea, a Cootie Bugs lesson also illustrates two crosscutting ideas that help to unify the different disciplines of science and engineering: systems and system models, and structure and function.

The first activity also integrates science with a branch of mathematics—logical reasoning involving sets and Venn diagrams. As indicated in the quote from the Common Core Standards, one of the mathematical practices that students are expected to learn is to construct viable arguments and critique the reasoning of others. So although it may at first appear to be just a science lesson, Cootie Bugs merges the disciplines of science and mathematics.

To try these activities with your students, for each small group of three to four students you will need:

- Two large sheets of butcher paper or chart paper and markers/crayons
- Science journals for each group to record observations and ideas
- Each group will need their own set of the two different cootie bugs pictures (available on page 85 and on the Heinemann website at www.heinemann.com/products/04358/.aspx—click on the Companion Resources tab).

Teacher Information

To help clarify the traits found on the West and East Cootie Bugs, we have provided the follow information before you read the story to your students.

The West Cootie Bugs live in an environment that is very cold and windy with a great amount of precipitation throughout the year. The East Cootie Bugs live where it is much drier and warm most of the year. Therefore, both are very well adapted to their environments. One of the goals of the following activities is to help students think about how body characteristics enable animals to survive in their environment. The students are going to observe the cootie bug traits and then begin to formulate, as a group, what each body part might be used for and how it helps them survive. There is no right or wrong set of answers but the goal is to use the scientific practice of inquiry and inference (Figure 9.1).

Observing the Traits of Two Populations of Cooties

Before you pass out the pictures of the cootie bugs, tell the students the following story:

> Normally cooties are very tiny, but in order to find cootie bugs this big you have to travel to the majestic Sierra Nevada Mountain range in California and Nevada. The Sierra Nevada is divided into a western side and an eastward side.

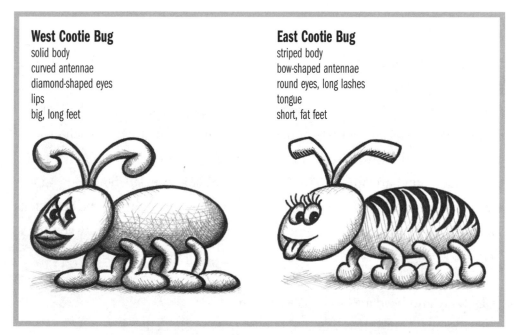

West Cootie Bug
solid body
curved antennae
diamond-shaped eyes
lips
big, long feet

East Cootie Bug
striped body
bow-shaped antennae
round eyes, long lashes
tongue
short, fat feet

Figure 9.1 West and East Cootie Bugs.

The western side of the mountain range is much colder and windier. The life-forms that live there have adapted to colder weather, where they receive most of their precipitation from falling snow. The east side of the mountain is much drier and warmer. The species who live on this side of the mountain have adapted to this drier and warmer climate.

The two groups of cootie bugs have lived on the opposite sides of the mountain range for thousands of years and have evolved into two different species that look very different from one another. The cootie bugs from the east side of the mountains where it is warmer and drier live mostly among the red sandstone rocks. These cootie bugs have striped body covering. They also have bow-shaped antennae, round eyes with long lashes, a very long tongue, and short, fat feet.

On the colder western side of the mountain, these cootie bugs live among the bluish granite rocks and have solid body coverings. Besides their different body coverings, these West Cootie Bugs have long curved antennae, diamond-shaped eyes, lips, and big, long feet.

You can see how these observable characteristics, or traits, that are very different help the bugs survive in their own environment. Why do you think they have different characteristics?

This would be a good time for the students to have a class discussion as they begin brainstorming their ideas for the differences before moving onto the next part of the activity.

Divide the class into small collaborative groups of three or four students. Pass out copies of the pictures of the two different cootie bugs to each group and ask the students to discuss in their groups the observable differences and how these body parts might have helped the West and East Cootie Bug survive in their environments. Ask one student in each group to be the recorder. They will find five observable physical characteristics, or traits, between the two cootie bugs.

1. Body and head are either solid or striped.
2. Antennae are either wide and curved or bow-shaped.

3. Eyes are either diamond-shaped or round with long lashes.

4. Mouths have either lips or tongues.

5. Feet are either big and long or short and fat.

As the students discuss the two different cootie bugs, they are to come to a group consensus on how the five observable traits help the cootie bugs be well suited for living in their environment. Remind the students to go back and think about the difference in the two environments on each side of the mountains. It might even help the students to draw a picture of what they think each environment looks like.

Once the small groups have come to agreement about the traits of the two populations of cootie bugs, summarize by having the students record their observations on a large sheet of butcher paper or chart paper, with two big circles, as shown in Figure 9.2.

Conclude this part of the activity by explaining that cooties are "true breeding" for these traits. That is, baby cootie bugs are always born with the same traits of their parents. If they did not have these traits, they probably would not survive in the habitat where they are found.

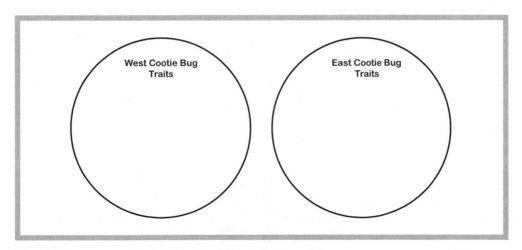

Figure 9.2 Diagram summarizing class observations of two cootie bug populations.

East Meets West

The next part of the lesson starts out with the following story:

> Recently researchers decided to put the two different cootie bugs together from the west and east regions. They wanted to see if they would reproduce. And to their great delight they did mate. After all they were both cootie bugs, they just looked different from one another. Now your task is to figure out what different traits the cootie bug babies might have with one parent from the east side and one from the west side of the Sierra Nevada Mountains. And would all the offspring look the same?

Divide the students into small groups. Assign each small group to come up with five traits of the new baby cootie bugs as a result of such a pairing. Once they have their five new traits, they need to draw what their new baby would look like. Then the group should think about what they want to tell the researchers who are trying to create a home for the baby cootie bug. This should be based on the characteristics of the habitat that would be needed for the baby cootie bug to survive.

Summarize the characteristics of the two East and West Cootie Bugs and their babies by using a diagram shown in Figure 9.3.

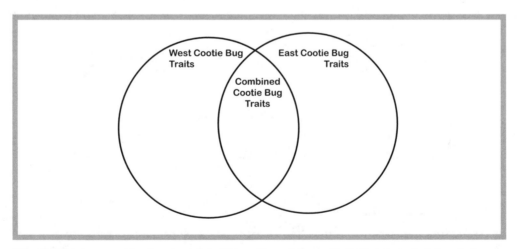

Figure 9.3 Diagram summarizing class observations of two cootie populations and traits of a baby cootie that results from a mating of cooties from two different populations.

Discussion

A key feature of the work of scientists, engineers, and mathematicians is scientific communication, which includes the practice of engaging in discourse with others. Having the students present and explain their ideas in front of their peers is part of the formal learning of how scientists work.

Encourage your students, as they listen to each others' presentations, to write down questions to ask the group that just presented. Did the combination of traits sound reasonable given the traits of the parents? Did they describe features of the habitat that the baby cootie bug would need to survive? If not what additional features would be needed?

Extensions of These Introductory Activities

Although these activities do not introduce natural selection and genetics, which are middle school science topics, if you are interested in extending these activities to those more sophisticated ideas, you can download a teacher guide for "Cootie Genetics" at the following website: http://biotech.bio5.org/jr_biotech#KootieGenetics. This website is the BIOTECH Project at the University of Arizona's Bio5 Institute.[1]

Concluding Thoughts

The Cootie Bugs unit is presented in this chapter as an example of an integrated STEM unit that combines ideas in life science (elementary concepts of adaptation and genetics) and mathematics (Venn diagrams). Consider the following comments about the interdisciplinary approach from Chapter 8. In what ways is the Cootie unit consistent with this approach? In what ways is it different?

In this approach to integration, teachers organize the curriculum around common learning across disciplines. They chunk together the common learning

---

[1] A special thanks to Dr. Nadja Anderson, BIOTECH Project Director at the University of Arizona, for giving us the overall idea for these activities. We encourage you to take the time to explore the BIOTECH website and search for JrBio5 Project for more information about Cootie Genetics and other biotechnology units such as Kiwi DNA Extraction, DNA Fingerprinting, DNA Origami, and Disease Detection.

embedded in the disciplines to emphasize interdisciplinary skills and concepts. The disciplines are identifiable, but they assume less importance than in the multidisciplinary approach. Therefore the first step in designing this type of STEM curriculum is to choose a key concept or skill that is important for all students to learn and that is enriched by combining knowledge and skills from two or more disciplines.

A second goal of this chapter has been to emphasize the importance of STEM practices. Students need experiences with the practice of communication and discourse with their peers. By engaging in activities like the Cootie Bugs lesson, for which there are no right or wrong answers but are nonetheless open to interpretation, will help your students gain self-confidence and improve their abilities to defend and debate their ideas.

Reflection

- Recall the ideas about STEM practices from the previous chapters. Can you see other STEM practices that are fostered through this activity?

- Are there other units that you currently teach that may involve the kind of logic and use of Venn diagrams in this unit? What other questions would you ask to stimulate your student's logical thinking?

REFERENCES

BIOTECH Project at the University of Arizona. 2009–2010. *Cootie Genetics*. Bio5 Institute, University of Arizona. Available at: http://biotech.bio5.org/jr_biotech#KootieGenetics.

Common Core State Standards Initiative. *Common Core Standards in Mathematics*. Available at: www.corestandards.org/the-standards/mathematics/.

West Cootie Bug

East Cootie Bug

10

A Pig's Tale

The following is Cary Snei-der's recollection of how he used all three approaches to integrated STEM education during one of his first years as a teacher.

BEFORE READING THIS CHAPTER,

think about your own first or second year of teaching. What comes to mind? What kept you in the teaching profession?

There is sufficient evidence with regard to achievement, inter-est, and motivation benefits associated with new integrative STEM instructional approaches to warrant further implementa-tion and investigation of those new approaches. Seasoned ed-ucators understand the importance of interest and motivation in learning, constructs validated by the findings of cognitive scientists over the past three decades. It follows, therefore, that integrative STEM instruction, implemented throughout the P–12 curriculum, has potential for greatly increasing the per-centage of students who become interested in STEM subjects and STEM fields.

—"STEM, STEM Education, STEMmania,"
in *The Technology Teacher*, Sanders (2009, 22–23)

The Setting

Costa Rica Academy was one of my first teaching jobs. It was a small parent-owned school in San Juan, the capital of Costa Rica in Central America. Known worldwide for its excellent coffee, Costa Rica is bordered by Nicaragua on the north and Panama on the south and stretches between the Atlantic and Pacific Oceans. It is a stable democracy with no standing army. During presidential elections, the entire country is alive with parades and banners and speeches.

Costa Rica Academy was an exciting place for a young science teacher who wanted to experience living in a different part of the world. I was the Chair of the middle school science department—a department of one—for two fabulous years. I also taught math and social studies on occasion, because we were a small school, just 250 students K–12. At one time we counted students from eighteen different countries. The language of instruction was Spanish (in art and PE) and English (in math, science, language arts, and social studies).

Our faculty of five (four in the second year after budget cuts) met once a week to discuss our eighty students in grades 5 through 8 and to share ideas. Most of the time we did our own thing, relying on our experience, purchasing most instructional materials from the United States, but using local materials and engaging our students in the life of the country whenever we could. And although we weren't aware of the three forms of integrative teaching described in Chapter 8, we were nonetheless aware that collaborating was a good idea, so that our students could see how what they learned in one class was connected to what they learned in the other classes.

As I look back over those two years, I can recall many formative experiences in my own education as a teacher. For example, I can picture Janet and Marion, two very bright sixth graders, who would always challenge me when I introduced a new topic. I can hear their voices in unison say, "Why do we have to do this, Mr. Sneider?" To this day, whether I'm teaching children or graduate students, I always come to class prepared to explain why what I'm about to teach is relevant—from the students' point of view. I also recall three curriculum units that illustrate the three different kinds of integrative teaching described in Chapter 8.

Multidisciplinary Teaching: Field Trip to a Volcano

In addition to the mild climate, plentiful sun, and adequate, predictable rainfall, the real secret of Costa Rica's excellent coffee is soil enriched with volcanic ash. The soil is so rich, in fact, that a stick freshly cut from a tree will grow when stuck into the ground. The easiest way to build a fence is to place several sticks in a row, wait a while for them to grow into small trees, then string wire between them, thereby creating one of Costa Rica's famous "living fences."

During each of the two years I taught at Costa Rica Academy, the entire middle school spent a full week at Aranal, one of two volcanoes on the Meseta Central, the large high plateau in the middle of the country. Aranal is a dormant volcano—at least when we were there—a popular place for tourists and summer camp experiences for kids. We rented one of the camps for a week and packed the buses with teaching materials, food, and kids for the relatively short trip to a gentle slope on the lower flank of the mountain.

We spent several weeks planning activities that we would carry out that week. Our goal each year was to plan activities that related to our locale. I taught a mapping unit in which students would use compasses, levels, and long measuring sticks to measure the extent and slope of the area, then create a papier-mâché relief map of our campsite. We led the students on hikes to identify flora and fauna, and we speculated about the source of the water in the small streams we forded. We built mud ovens for cooking, like those made by the Indians who lived there before the Spanish conquests. We also did a number of craft activities, including kite building and quilt making and campfire skits that had little to do with the volcano, except that they seemed to fit the location.

Looking back on the experience today, I could have done a unit on tectonics and had the students draw what they imagined lay underneath the volcano and had them collect and identify rocks, looking for signs of volcanism, using one of the excellent units in which students figure out how the rock was formed by observing its structure. We would also have created a timeline for the various volcanic eruptions known to have occurred on the Meseta Central over the past 10,000 years, imagining what it would have been like to live there at the time. Nonetheless, I think the activities that were most closely related to our locale fit the definition of a multidisciplinary (thematic) unit as described in Chapter 8:

> The multidisciplinary, or thematic, approach connects the individual disciplines by organizing the curriculum around a common theme such as "Oceans," "Ecosystems," "Flight," or "Pirates." This approach is used to provide coherence to the curriculum so that the students have an opportunity to see that they can learn about something in many different ways.

Interdisciplinary Teaching: Geodesic Cities

I've always been fascinated by architecture; and shortly before leaving for Costa Rica I purchased a book about geodesic domes. While reading the book, an idea came to me for a unit that would merge my math teaching with the building of structures—what today I would call construction technology. I'm not sure I had the entire unit planned beforehand, as I recall it grew over a period of about six to eight weeks of daily lessons.

Math: We started with the five regular geometric solids, using a simple activity to determine which of the solids is stable when it is constructed of just edges, made with straws and string. I showed the students how to slip a string through a soda straw, and tie them together into the five regular solids: tetrahedron, cube, pentagon, hexagon, and icosahedron (Figure 10.1).

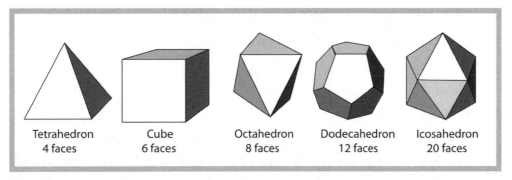

| Tetrahedron | Cube | Octahedron | Dodecahedron | Icosahedron |
| 4 faces | 6 faces | 8 faces | 12 faces | 20 faces |

Figure 10.1 Five regular solids.

Some of these structures were stable—they kept their shape when released—and others collapsed.

Technology: I then showed the students pictures of several different structures—rectangular buildings like most they were familiar with, conical teepees, igloos, yurts, and geodesic domes—and asked them which they thought were most stable, based on the activity they just did and to identify what about the structures created the stability. They had little difficulty seeing the triangles in the tetrahedron and icosahedron (the only two stable structures) providing the stability that was needed. Although we didn't use the word technology as I would today, the students discussed how these different traditional building technologies probably evolved, by experimenting with local materials and just playing with shapes (as they did with straws and strings) to make something that didn't collapse. In other words, people in many different cultures discovered basic properties of the geometric solids and figured out how to use those properties to change the natural environment to meet their needs.

Engineering: I still have the activity sheets that I developed and distributed on ditto paper, in which I asked the students to write their ideas about why people today would build rectangular houses. They had some good ideas. For example, a rectangular solid is a convenient shape to pack into a city laid out in square blocks, easy to make with straight boards, and so on. Then I stated the challenge: Use more straws and string to build a rectangular structure that stands up by itself, which could serve as a framework for a house. They had little trouble figuring out that they needed to add crosspieces to their cubes not only to make a sloping roof but also to strengthen the walls. I remember that they were a creative group, and their houses were not exactly alike.

History: At this point we were halfway to geodesic domes. We had triangles. The next step was the arch. I went back to the local bookstore and found a book on European architecture. The pictures I found led us to the unit on bridges. We looked at lots of different bridges, talked about the simplest bridges that the earliest people would have created (a log across a stream), and marveled at the aqueducts built by the Romans. We also looked at pictures of Romanesque and Gothic churches and discussed the various structures that people developed over time to create the structures that they not only needed but were also innovative, beautiful, and that allowed them to express artistic and religious ideas. Today we look back on architecture as one of the major ways to characterize historical and cultural periods.

Innovation: We discussed the advantages of arches, though I don't recall building them. We did, however, take a field trip to see Costa Rica's famous "upside-down bridge," with the arch on the bottom, as a supporting structure. It is an odd kind of suspension bridge across a very deep ravine. Cables are hung from the banks so they drape in a parabolic arc. The cables are then encased in concrete and concrete pillars are built on top of the arc. A roadway is then built across the top of the pillars. It is a beautiful structure but counterintuitive as it is not immediately obvious how it stands up. It's just the sort of puzzle that science teachers love. I don't remember if the students figured it out right away, but I do remember showing them pictures of how the bridge was built, starting with the cables laid across the ravine. Seeing those cables was a sufficient clue for them to envision how the structure functioned to hold up the roadway. The point of the lesson was the importance of innovation in engineering—thinking of new ways to apply existing technologies.

Technology and Math: For the transition from arches to domes, we went back to the history books to see images of the Roman pantheon and a number of church domes. The students could easily see how they could take an arch and rotate it about a vertical axis to create a dome. Again it provided more insight into the relationship between mathematics and technology, though I was probably not as articulate as I hope I would be today in describing the concept of axis of symmetry and how rotations of different shapes can be used to create three-dimensional structures. Nonetheless, the relationship between the arch and the dome is sufficiently obvious that the concepts were clear enough.

Architecture: At that point, I introduced Buckminster Fuller and how he fused the idea of the triangle and the dome to invent a kind of structure that was very strong (because it was made out of triangles) and could span large spaces (because it was in the shape of a dome). There were no local sources of kits for building domes, so I cased the local hardware stores and came up with the least expensive source of dome materials: welding rods and small nuts and bolts. I went through many hacksaw blades cutting welding rods to three different lengths, flattening the ends with a hammer, and drilling holes at both ends. The students sanded off rough edges and worked in teams to assemble their eighteen-inch-diameter domes. Each team was assigned a function for their structure (apartment building, schools, stores, police or fire station, library, businesses of various sorts) and designed and built the interior using cardboard for the various floors.

City Planning: The last step was city planning. I had four classes of students. Each class laid out a plan, with ideas for making the city as livable as possible, so people would not need to travel too far from their homes to market or to work, have places for play outdoors on the weekends, and so on. The students looked at each others' plans and the entire middle school gradually came to consensus. In retrospect it was an engineering task, because we needed to take the needs of the city dwellers into account as we systematically compared four different solutions. We pulled all of the tables in the room together, and created our city—ending what was for me, and I hope for at least some of my students, my second-most memorable teaching unit during the two years I lived and worked in Costa Rica.

This unit was intentionally planned as an interdisciplinary unit. As described in Chapter 8:

In this [interdisciplinary] approach to integration, teachers organize the curriculum around common learning goals across disciplines. They chunk together the common learning embedded in the disciplines to emphasize interdisciplinary skills and concepts. The disciplines are identifiable, but they assume less importance than in the multidisciplinary approach. Therefore, the first step in designing this type of STEM curriculum is to choose a key concept or skill that is important for all students to learn and that is enriched by combining knowledge and skills from two or more disciplines.

Transdisciplinary Teaching: Life and Times of Willie the Pig

My favorite unit turned out to be the one I feared most. Because my educational and earlier teaching experiences were in astronomy and physical science, I was worried about teaching biology. But I had little choice. In addition to recognizing that our students needed a well-balanced science curriculum, the headmaster was a zealous biology teacher who would stop at every roadkill for an on-the-spot dissection of a rattlesnake or whatever he and his family encountered.

Following in my headmaster's footsteps, I started with dissection. Unable to afford prepared specimens and nearly defeated by a misadventure with our local toads, to which my students loudly objected, it occurred to me that an easy approach would be to have them dissect chickens. Because our school cooks normally cleaned the chickens, it was simply a matter of offering to help them by having the students dissect the chickens between plucking and cooking. It worked exceptionally well, and I remember the students were absolutely amazed by how long a chicken's intestines were. I doubt if we could have done this in the United States, but at a small school in Costa Rica, there were no objections and my headmaster couldn't have been more pleased.

The unit was interdisciplinary in a small way as I invited an artist to present a lesson on how to sketch the unfolding dissection. She demonstrated how to start with simple shapes that represent the basic outlines of the animal and then gradually fill in details. The art teacher's objective was for the students to learn to draw what they see, starting with the big picture, then observing and drawing finer and finer details. As the science teacher, my objective was for the students to observe the internal structures of an organism to gain insight into how their own bodies functioned. Our objectives were complementary, so the unit could be described as interdisciplinary.

The next step was to introduce one more specimen for the dissection unit so the students could compare the differences in the internal structures of two different organisms. But my plans to extend the unit shifted when I (willingly) gave way to my students' concerns. Here's what happened.

When I explained to the students that we would end the unit with another dissection, one of my students, whose parents owned a pig farm, offered to bring in a runt from the current litter for dissection. To prepare for this new challenge, I went to the bookstore to find a book on dissecting pigs, as I had done before starting the chicken dissections. I used my Spanish phrase book and went from bookstore to bookstore, and all I got were smiles and shakes of the head. Then one of the other teachers told me that the language I used to ask for the book "para dissection del chancho" meant in Costa Rican dialect "for dissecting a dirty filthy person." I eventually found a book about the innards of a "cerdo," the proper word for *pig*, but before I had a chance to use it my student brought in the runt, and the unit took a major new turn.

When Brad carried the little pig, alive and kicking, into the classroom, the girls immediately fell in love with it and took turns holding it. Later that day, I found out from the English teacher that the kids were outraged that "mean Mr. Sneider" was going to kill the piglet for no good reason at all! The boy who brought it in and most of the other boys thought killing and dissecting the pig sounded like a fine idea. So the English teacher marched over to the science lab and arranged for a stay of execution while she organized a debate the next day.

I didn't get to attend the debate because I had to teach science while it was taking place, but I got the details later. The consensus of opinion was that the girls won, as at least some of the boys came over to their side. Although I agreed to let the pig live, I challenged the students to help me solve two problems that stemmed from this decision. First, we needed to house, feed, and otherwise care for the pig. Second, we needed to acknowledge the generous parents who donated the pig to our school by finding a way to use the pig in our science program. Because we weren't going to dissect the pig, how else might we use it to learn science?

To solve the first problem, I assigned some of the students to get tools and materials from the school carpenter and to design and build a pig pen. To make a long story short, the pen, which they built and rebuilt several times, suggested the name for the pig. As a consequence of their history lessons about the settling of the U.S. Colonies, they named the pig after William Penn, and put up a sign: "Willi's Pen" (Figure 10.2). The cafeteria staff helped with the food, because there was nearly always leftover salad after lunch. Also, most of them raised pigs at home, so they had good ideas to suggest for maintaining the pig's health.

To solve the second problem, the students suggested that the cute little pig, now named "Willie," could help us do animal behavior experiments. As this was long before the Internet, the students needed my help in researching what these experiments might be. I went back to the bookstore and found an excellent book on animal behavior. I explained Pavlov's experiments about getting a

Figure 10.2 Willie's Pen (Image by Cary Sneider).

dog to salivate at the ringing of a bell, and the students devised an experiment that somehow ended up with Willie ringing a bell by walking through a gate whenever he was hungry. So Willie succeeded in conditioning us to respond to the bell. Although the experiment did not go as planned, the students understood the concept of operant conditioning and realized how difficult it was to duplicate even a classic experiment like Pavlov's. Soon we turned to the next science unit about insect classification and behavior that involved a local beekeeper installing an observation beehive in our classroom.

As I look back on that series of lessons, I realize it was one of my first transdisciplinary classes. Remember, in the transdisciplinary approach, the teacher organizes the curriculum around student questions and concerns. The students' overriding concern for the life of the pig clearly caused me to rethink the unit. I realized that giving up the secondary objective of comparing the internal structures of two different organisms was a reasonable trade-off, given that I had a chance to capture the students' energy and enthusiasm for using the pig in a different way. But their energy needed to be channeled by a new curriculum plan.

Recall that in a transdisciplinary unit, an essential question is the driver, the STEM learning objectives provide the road map, and the students' prior experiences are the guideposts. In this case, the essential question was: How do we save this poor little pig? The first objective—to figure out how to house, feed, and care for the pig—involved research (talking to the cooks) and engineering design (building, repairing, and rebuilding Willie's pen). The second objective, learning how to conduct animal behavior experiments, also involved research to learn enough about animal behavior to formulate a research question and then how to plan, conduct, and analyze the results of an experiment. In the case of the second objective, we focused on controlling variables, recording the results of each trial, and drawing thoughtful and honest conclusions. I was satisfied that accomplishing these objectives was more important than the original objective associated with one more dissection.

Finally, in a transdisciplinary unit, the students' prior experiences are the guideposts as they work together on a real-world problem. My students came from many different countries and continents, including Costa Rica, Europe, Asia, Africa, and North and South America. They had different experiences and different ideas about animals and about science, which they shared as they struggled to solve the two challenges that stemmed from the decision to save Willie. I believe that their different experiences led not only to better solutions but also to a better appreciation of cultural differences—although they may not have expressed it in those terms. Working together, and with guidance from the teacher, the carpenter, and the kitchen staff, the students succeeded in solving some challenging real-world problems.

Concluding Thoughts

To conclude this journey down memory lane, I realize that I have always liked the idea of integrated STEM teaching, though I did not have the language to express it until recently. And recognizing that the three approaches to integrated teaching applied to my teaching experience in Costa Rica did not occur to me until I started working on this book!

So to recap: Our school visit to a volcano was an experience in *multidisciplinary* teaching, because our middle school team devised a variety of activities all related to the volcano, but not necessarily to each other. The Geodesic Cities unit was *interdisciplinary*, because it involved a fusion of mathematics and engineering. And our work with Willie the pig was *transdisciplinary*, because the curriculum was organized around student questions and concern and the students had to apply their knowledge and skills in a real-world context.

Reflection

- Think back over your life's experiences as a student or as a teacher. Can you recall an example of multidisciplinary teaching? Interdisciplinary teaching? Transdisciplinary teaching?

- If you can recall these incidents, which one made the greatest impression on you?

REFERENCE

Sanders, M. 2009. "STEM, STEM Education, STEMmania." *The Technology Teacher* (December/January).

CHAPTER 11

Giants and Borrowers

Practice 4: Mathematically proficient students can apply the mathematics they know to solve problems arising in everyday life, society, and the workplace. In early grades, this might be as simple as writing an addition equation to describe a situation. In middle grades, a student might apply proportional reasoning to plan a school event or analyze a problem in the community.

—*Common Core Standards in Mathematics.*
Online at http://www.corestandards.org/the-standards/mathematics

Following is Michael Comer's recollection of how he and his fellow middle school teachers coordinated their efforts to help students understand ratio and proportion.

BEFORE READING THE CHAPTER, think about how you use ratio and proportion in your daily life, such as figuring out how much of each ingredient you need when doubling or tripling a recipe.

The Challenge

The seventh-grade class had just come in from math. The students were talking about the launch of the Mars Rover mission. They couldn't fathom why it would take so long for the rocket to reach Mars. If the rocket was traveling so fast, why would it take over seven months for it to get to Mars? Juan was arguing that if they could build faster rockets they could get there sooner, but Marco was defending his position that no matter how fast the rocket travels, the planet was always moving and it's hard for a rocket to catch up with the planet while it is moving through space.

This discussion reminded me of how difficult it is for many students to visualize the vast distances that span our solar system. I should not have been surprised because large numbers can be overwhelming to students and adults alike. We trifle at the Department of Defense spending of 665 *billion* dollars or the size of the national debt at 14 *trillion*. It is amazing that the public at large has a hard time visualizing the difference that a few extra zeros in a number truly mean. The perception that the movement of the decimal point one way or another is "not that big a deal" has always amazed me.

At that time I was planning the next unit—one that I always had trouble getting students to understand—ratio and proportion. For example, take the ratio 1:4, which can also be expressed as $^1/_4$, or "one-quarter." It's easy enough to understand what $^1/_4$ cup of water means; but it's harder to see that the same ratio expresses the relationship between a quarter and a dollar, or 2.5 million people out of a population of 10 million.

Rates, such as miles per hour, are similar to ratios because they involve division of one number by another. The only difference is that rates involve the division of two numbers with different units, and ratios usually refer to division of two numbers with the same units, so specifying the units is not necessary.

Proportional reasoning is even more difficult because it involves comparing two ratios. For example, the discussion of gear ratios in Chapter 6 concerned proportional reasoning because students were expected to realize that the ratio of turns between two meshed gears was the same as the ratio of the number of teeth on the two gears. As a pure math problem this is usually called "equivalent fractions," but it's the same idea as proportional reasoning.

At the regular middle school team meeting that day I brought up the Mars Rover discussion, eliciting sympathetic groans from the other teachers. We also discussed how few of the students understood mathematics concepts or how mathematics related to their daily lives.

STEM LESSON ESSENTIALS • Integrating Science, Technology, Engineering, and Mathematics

During that meeting an idea came to us. What if we coordinated our efforts and provided activities that incorporated the mathematics in some way and related to the subject areas they normally taught? Would using numbers in different situations help the students grasp the concepts and see the practical application of the mathematics? That was the beginning of a multidisciplinary unit we called Travel.

Multidisciplinary Teaching: Travel

The middle school team decided that for the next two weeks we would all concentrate on using the concepts of rates, ratios, proportion, and scale in the work we were doing in our classes. The math teacher's role was to provide the basic instruction in the mathematics concepts. As the science teacher, I would teach the students how to measure speed, and the social studies and language arts teachers would focus on the application of these ideas in their subjects.

In social studies the students learned about the early pioneers moving westward across the Great Plains. Like other early explorers, Lewis and Clark kept meticulous notes of their travels. Using some of these data, the students mapped out the route they took as they explored the Louisiana Territory. Using this information, the students were able to calculate the average speed of their journey as they moved from one location to another. In an important sense, the first trips across the continent in covered wagons were similar in time and space to crossing the vast distance between the planets in a spacecraft—but only if viewed as a comparison of ratios.

As their social studies class continued, the students learned that new forms of travel had an important impact on the success of moving people across the Great Plains from the East to the West. The covered wagon and Pony Express gave way to the steam locomotive and the rise of the railroad system. Students had to calculate the speed at which travel changed from 1810 to 1900 with the development of the railroad system. The steam locomotive and the Pullman sleeper made travel across the Great Plains easier. The telegraph enabled faster and better communications with the West. Improvements in photography and printing made stories and images of the West more accessible to more people in the crowded cities of the East.

In language arts, students read excerpts from the journals and diaries that reflected the opinions and ideas at the time. They read from the books of Laura Ingalls Wilder depicting life on the Great Plains. These readings provided a backdrop for understanding how difficult it was for the people living there and how the available means of transportation affected people's lives. Students created their own journal entries and compared their lives with the people and events in the books they read. The next step was to write persuasive composi-tions about the effects of technological advances in transportation on society and to create arguments both for and against the settlement of the West. The students created rate tables depicting the population growth of major cities to support their arguments.

In this integrated approach, the individual subjects remained intact, but there was a connection that the students experienced as they moved from one class to another. Ideas and skills developed in mathematics and science classes were applied in social studies and language arts. Although some of the connec-tions may have been a bit contrived, it helped the students appreciate that the work they did in one class had value in another. That is an important advantage of the multidisciplinary approach, as described in Chapter 8:

> The multidisciplinary, or thematic, approach connects the individual dis-ciplines by organizing the curriculum around a common theme such as "Oceans," "Ecosystems," "Flight," or "Pirates." This approach is used to provide coherence to the curriculum so that the students have an opportunity to see that they can learn about something in many different ways.

Interdisciplinary Teaching: Ratio and Proportion

Although the middle school unit on Travel is perhaps best described as multi-disciplinary, the science and mathematics classes were truly interdisciplinary. The math teacher based his examples and problem sets around modes of transportation and included technologies like Maglev trains, supersonic transport, and Formula One race cars. This complemented the science class in which students compare the top speed of a wide range of vehicles that work on different scientific principles.

In science, the core concepts introduced in the mathematics class were appropriate for the unit on force and motion. The students worked with toy cars and ramps and learned how to measure distance and time and how to calculate the speed of any moving object. They also measured the rate at which the speed changed as the cars sped up or slowed down. The ability to calculate speed and compare rates of change demonstrated the students' abilities to apply the concepts of rate and ratio that they learned in math class.

The math teacher and I worked closely together to coordinate math instruction with the students' science explorations. As the students generated and collected data from their science class, the math teacher helped them analyze the information as part of the math class. In this way, students had the advantage of using real-world and relevant information in a way that made sense to them.

This close collaboration best fits the definition of interdisciplinary teaching as described in Chapter 8:

> In this [interdisciplinary] approach to integration, teachers organize the curriculum around common learning goals across disciplines. They chunk together the common learning embedded in the disciplines to emphasize interdisciplinary skills and concepts. The disciplines are identifiable, but they assume less importance than in the multidisciplinary approach. Therefore, the first step in designing this type of STEM curriculum is to choose a key concept or skill that is important for all students to learn and that is enriched by combining knowledge and skills from two or more disciplines.

Transdisciplinary Teaching: Size Matters

Although the Travel unit helped the students better understand rates and ratios, we were not entirely convinced that the students were able to apply proportional reasoning, which involves a comparison of two ratios. More importantly, we weren't convinced that the mathematical concepts that the students had gained so far were actually *enduring understandings*—that when faced with a future problem that could be solved using these concepts, students would naturally apply their new knowledge and skills; they did not yet see these ideas as something they would use in everyday life as a way to reason about situations that puzzled them or tasks they wanted to accomplish. From their perspective, ratio and proportion were not yet relevant and meaningful ways to reason about the world.

One of the Standards of Mathematical Practice in the Common Core State Standards calls for students to focus their attention on the thinking process of mathematics and not just the mechanical computation work that most students associate with school math. The math teacher agonized about how to help his students accomplish that level of understanding of ratio and proportion. "I need a 'hook'—something to stimulate *their* questions, that would naturally lead to applications of ratio and proportion to something they would find interesting," he said.

One of the topics that we heard the students talking about with some interest was the idea of "giants" and "little people." Fairy tales make use of both extremes of body size to illustrate points of view or make political statements. The giant—as in *Gulliver's Travels* (Swift 1892) or the English folktale "Jack and the Beanstalk" (Jacobs 1890)—gives students the impression of bigness. At the same time, there are stories of elves and leprechauns, people tiny in size that live in the world too. Thumbelina and Tom Thumb represent such characters in these fables. So one day the math teacher decided to build on the students' natural interest in these characters as a means for helping them develop the enduring understandings that were the real targets of the unit.

The conversation that sparked the unit was a discussion about what it would be like to be either a giant or tiny person. A small group of students were trying to figure out which was better, whether it was most advantageous to be a giant or to be tiny. One of the students said it was obvious that being smaller was better: "Just look at the dinosaurs," she said. "If bigger was better, why are there no dinosaurs today? The smaller animals lived and the larger ones died." This got the discussion going even more. What would be better, to be a giant in the world or to be a tiny person? With this remark, the beginnings of a mathematics unit on giants and Borrowers was started.

The recently released movie *The Secret Life of Arrietty* is a Japanese animated fantasy film based on Mary Norton's juvenile fantasy novel *The Borrowers* (Norton 1952). The film tells the story of Arrietty, a young "Borrower" who lives under the floorboards of a typical household. The story may be familiar to many, as there have been several screen adaptations of the Norton book, including one with John Goodman in 1997. Borrowers are only four inches tall. They coexist in our homes, making use of our objects and possessions, explaining such mysteries as missing socks in a finished batch of laundry.

To keep the focus on the students' interests, the teacher gave them an assignment in which they had opportunities to be creative—but that also required them to apply their new knowledge of ratio and proportion. The students could create a piece of scale model furniture befitting either a giant or a Borrower. They would become "household design engineers." They would have to develop a blueprint showing how they crafted their piece of furniture and provide a detailed record showing all of their converted measurements. This record would be part of the evaluation tool for the completion of the unit. It would show their proficiency in measuring and making and using scale drawings (another use of ratios).

"But how would we do that?" one of the students asked. "Would we need some directions or a blueprint for the model? How would we know it was the right size? How would we know if those items are correct?"

Rather than answering their questions, a discussion was launched in which the students made the choice of where to begin. We started with the giants. After some discussion, the students agreed that our giant would be fifteen feet tall (approximately 450 cm). To make the measurements easier to work with, they would use centimeters as our unit of linear measurement. The students were asked how they could determine how big the giant's foot was.

After more discussion, the teacher directed the students to take some measurements. "Do you think we all have about the same size foot?" "No!" they said. "We all have different size feet. Some of us have larger feet, some smaller." He asked them if they thought the length of the foot was in proportion to their height.

From this question, we began the investigation. They agreed to measure the left foot as a standard, and height without shoes. The teacher used his own foot and height as an example to demonstrate how the students should conduct their measurements. With the help of one of the students, they found that the teacher's foot was 30 cm long and his height was found to be 180 cm. Then the students worked in pairs to measure their own feet and height. They created a chart of the information and used an Excel spreadsheet to organize the data. Using the Excel formulas, they discovered that the ratio of the length of our foot to our height was approximately 1:6. It was pretty similar for almost everyone in the class.

If we thought the giant had the same body proportions as we do, then how long would his foot be? How about other body dimensions? From here the teacher reminded the students of the idea of ratio. "If the shape of a giant is directly proportional to one of us, then the ratio of his foot to his height should also be 1:6. So how would we find the length of the giant's foot?"

"Easy," said one of the students. "Take the giant's height and divide it by six. This should give us the length of his foot."

"How do you know that?" the teacher asked.

"Well the ratio's gotta be the same. It's like solving for a missing number in our division problems. If the length of the giant's foot in centimeters is X, and the giant's height is 450 cm, then:

$$1:6 = X:450 \text{ (1 to 6 equals } X \text{ to 450)}$$
$$X = (450/6) \text{ cm} = 75 \text{ cm}$$

"So the length of the giant's foot would be 75 cm? That's almost $2\frac{1}{2}$ feet long?" To illustrate the idea of comparisons, the students traced their own foot on

STEM LESSON ESSENTIALS • Integrating Science, Technology, Engineering, and Mathematics

paper and then made a drawing of the length of the giant's foot showing the difference between the length of their foot and that of the giant (Figure 11.1).

They measured other body parts and found some additional ratios:

- The length of our foot is approximately the same as the length of our forearm.
- The circumference of our fist is about the same as the length of our foot.
- The length of our forearm is about the same as the distance from our chin to the top of our head.
- The length of our face is about $^{1}/_{8}$ our height.
- The circumference of our head at the eyebrows is about $^{1}/_{3}$ our height.
- The distance around our wrist is twice the length of our thumb.
- The distance around our neck is twice the circumference of our wrist.

The teacher asked the students to use these measurements to calculate how big the giant's body would be using the same ratios. The students had data to

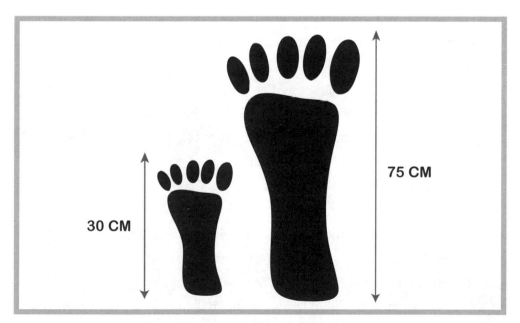

30 CM

75 CM

Figure 11.1 Ratio of our foot to a giant's foot.

work with and a meaningful experience in which to do the conversions. They then sketched the size of the giant on butcher paper, comparing the class' body measurement data with that of our giant.

The students then took these comparisons and related them to the size of the "little people"—the Borrowers. The students had to figure out the ratio between the measurements we knew to find the one we were missing. For example, they knew that Borrowers were approximately 4 inches tall. To use the same methods they used for the giants, they first needed to find the Borrower's height in centimeters. From the previous class the students know that the length of a human foot is about 12 inches, or about 30 centimeters. So the students were able to set up the problem like a language analogy: 12 is to 30 as 4 is to ? Or, $^{12}/_{30} = ^4/_?$. In this case, many of them were able to recognize 12 as a multiple of 4 and that the missing quantity had to be a factor of 30. (One student came up with the answer quickly. She used the dual scales on the measuring tape to see that 4 inches was equal to 10 cm!)

The building of the model furniture proved to be the most exciting. In this, students became engineers—taking the measurements they had gathered and through the design process created models of furniture consistent with what they would find in their own homes. They used a variety of materials, including foam packing pieces from a local appliance store, lunchroom drinking straws, wooden skewers, and modeling clay. Our furniture included a bedroom set complete with dresser, nightstand, and bed. A dining chair of PVC pipe to seat the giant overshadowed the miniature living room set (complete with stereo and television) designed for our Borrowers.

As the teacher looked back on the experiences that his students shared, it was clear that the high level of engagement would not only result in deeper knowledge but also provide the enduring understandings that had relevance to their personal interests. It was more than something they learned to get a good grade. The math teacher had the feeling that the ideas of ratio and proportion were becoming tools that they would be able to use in the future for understanding

STEM LESSON ESSENTIALS • Integrating Science, Technology, Engineering, and Mathematics

and modeling relationships and creating useful models for such tasks as drawing a map for directions or laying out furniture in their own room at home.

As we reflect on this experience, does it clearly meet the description of a transdisciplinary teaching approach as described in Chapter 8?

> In the transdisciplinary approach to integration, teachers organize curriculum around student questions and concerns. This is where we ask students to take ownership of the learning and they apply their interdisciplinary and disciplinary skills in a real-world context. In the transdisciplinary approach, the relevance of the students' learning and their ability to use their knowledge in a real-world application becomes the focal point. The essential question is the driver, the STEM learning objectives are the road map, and the students' previous experiences are the guideposts.

Concluding Thoughts

The unit on ratio and proportional reasoning that I describe in this chapter did not happen during the first year of teaching or the second or third year. The multidisciplinary unit on Travel was a major step forward, and it gave us a chance to collaborate with each other—which was very enjoyable for us as teachers and for our students. The interdisciplinary unit deepened the collaboration between the math teacher and me and helped many of our students overcome the cognitive barriers to understanding the concepts. Also, applying the same concept in several different contexts gave the students excellent practice in applying their mathematical skills. Finally, the transdisciplinary approach enabled the math teacher to harness the power of the students' interests and develop truly enduring understandings that would serve them well in life.

Reflection

- Consider the transitions from multidisciplinary to interdisciplinary to transdisciplinary teaching. What are your thoughts about these three approaches?

- Which approach are you most comfortable with?

- Which do you think is most engaging for students?

REFERENCES

Common Core State Standards Initiative. Mathematics. 2010. National Governors Association Center for Best Practices and Council of Chief State School Officers. Available at: www .corestandards.org/the-standards/mathematics/.

Jacobs, J. 1890. "Jack and the Beanstalk." In *English Fairy Tales*. The story is a folktale published by various authors. Jacobs' is one of the best-known early editions. New York: Dover Publishing Inc.

Norton, M. 1952. *The Borrowers*. London: Dent. 2003 paperback edition published by Houghton Mifflin Harcourt. *The Borrowers* was followed by a series of sequels recounting the further adventures of the Clock family:
- *The Borrowers Afield* (first published in 1955)
- *The Borrowers Afloat* (first published in 1959)
- *The Borrowers Aloft* (first published in 1961), which includes "Poor Stainless" (a story from Homily's childhood)
- *The Borrowers Avenged* (first published in 1982)

Swift, J. 1892. *Gulliver's Travels into Several Remote Nations of the World*. London: George Bell and Sons. Available at: www.gutenberg.org/files/829/829-h/829-h.htm.

CHAPTER 12

Project-Based Learning

Engineering literacy is the understanding of how technologies are developed via the engineering design process; lessons are project-based *and integrate multiple subjects, making difficult concepts relevant and tangible to students and tapping into students' natural interest in* problem-solving.

—"Innovate America: Building a Science, Technology, Engineering, Math Agenda,"
National Governor's Association (2007, 7)

> **BEFORE READING THIS CHAPTER,** recall ways that you or someone you know or heard about asked students to envision a real-world situation to establish a meaningful context for a lesson. How did the approach affect the ways that students engaged in the lesson and what they learned from it?

Project-Based + Problem-Solving = Transdisciplinary Learning

The last few chapters discussed a number of ways that teachers have combined the STEM fields with each other and with other subjects, stretching across the entire curriculum. Although different approaches resonate with different students, one of the most powerful is a form of transdisciplinary learning that builds on students' ideas and interests. In the previous two chapters, we saw an example of a transdisciplinary science lesson that started with students' desire to preserve the life of a piglet and another in which a math teacher built a unit on ratio and proportion by leveraging students' interests in "little people" and "giants." Both examples required that teachers notice connections between their students' interests and questions and curriculum goals, a situation that depends on a combination of teaching skill and serendipity. This chapter concerns a different transdisciplinary approach—project-based learning (PBL)—that doesn't require serendipity and that can be planned well in advance.

PBL is defined in a number of ways by different authors. In our view, effective project-based lessons must have at least three components: (1) *an essential question*, which establishes a real-world meaningful context and becomes the driver of student engagement; (2) standards-based *STEM learning objectives*, which provide the road map or direction; and (3) students' previous experiences that act as the guideposts through the learning experience. There are also other common characteristics of project-based lessons. For example, they often take place over a longer period than most lessons, involve the creative solution to a problem, and usually result in a tangible product. Later in the chapter, we will expand on these qualities and describe additional characteristics of PBL. First, however, let's look at an example.

Example of a PBL Unit

This fifth-sixth grade unit called "Where Is Away?" is based on helping students think about where their trash goes when they throw something "away." The unit starts from science objectives (understanding renewable and nonrenewable resources and the impact of using those resources) but includes objectives from math, technology, engineering, language arts, and social studies. The unit engages students in doing research on waste management, landfills, and recycling with a major goal around encouraging them to become socially responsible citizens for their school, the home, the Earth, and its resources. (The following ideas are adapted from a middle school chemistry unit from the CEPUP series *The Waste Hierarchy: "Where is Away?"* 1993.[1])

---

[1]*The Waste Hierarchy: Where Is "Away?"* was developed by the Lawrence Hall of Science, University of California at Berkeley, and published by Addison-Wesley as part of a series by the Chemical Education for Public Understanding Program (CEPUP). This unit is copyrighted by The Regents of the University of California and used with permission. The series has since expanded to include issue-oriented curricula in a variety of science fields, and is now the SEPUP program (www.sepuplhs.org), with materials and kits published by Lab-Aids (http://lab-aids.com). *The Waste Hierarchy: Where Is "Away?"* was revised and published in 2003 as Waste Disposal: *Computers and the Environment.*

STEM LESSON ESSENTIALS • Integrating Science, Technology, Engineering, and Mathematics

The students have been learning about the increasing amount of garbage people produce and how their local community landfill is running out of space. They decided that it would be an excellent idea to become "student waste management consultants" who could be hired to evaluate their school and community recycling/waste management practices.

The students began their project by analyzing just how much waste their own school produced and how much of it was recycled. They then worked in teams to develop a new schoolwide recycling plan complete with a cost analysis and supporting data to propose recommendations to their parents, teachers, administrators, and school board members. The teams developed a slideshow and brochures to inform the other students, teachers, and families of their school to help persuade them to take action. They even designed a Web page for their school site that promoted recycling at home. In a final show of social responsibility, students turned some of the trash into treasures as they diverted non-recyclable material from the school wastebaskets and turned them into attractive merchandise to sell at a holiday fair.

This PBL unit can take a number of different directions, depending on the teacher's decisions and student responses. The teacher can start by posing an essential question: "Where is away?" This essential question could serve as the springboard for a PBL unit that might start by breaking down the problem into manageable chunks: Where has all the trash gone in the past? How can we figure out how much it costs to get rid of our trash? How are different materials (plastic, glass, paper, and so forth) recycled? How can we learn how people feel about recycling?

Guidance for the students will derive from standards-based STEM learning objectives. For example, this class might focus on objectives requiring them to use electronic resources to gather information and communicate that information, as well as understanding the technologies involved in waste disposal.

Science objectives might begin with a study on renewable and nonrenewable resources and involve environmental impacts related to humans' use and disposal of resources.

The math objectives might include statistical analysis of the data students collect about trash disposal, recycling, and people's attitudes about recycling and the preparation of a cost analysis.

Engineering objectives would be relevant to answering the essential question by applying engineering design practices, such as defining the problem to be solved in terms of criteria and constraints, generating a variety of different ideas for reducing the amount of non-recycled waste, and using a systematic method for comparing the different ideas to determine which would make the biggest difference; testing the leading ideas; and working as a team to communicate their best ideas.

Additional learning objectives could also be developed for social studies and English language arts. These could include "conducting research to build and present knowledge" and the "production of clear, coherent writings appropriate to the task and audience" (CCSS-ELA 2010). The development of such objectives is essential if the students are expected to work on the project during time designated for these other subjects.

The students' previous experiences determine how they will work together to investigate the problem. The teacher might take the class on a field trip to a local landfill to build background knowledge. Some students might begin by looking for sources of trash in the school. Others might create logs of student paper usage, interview the principal about the amount spent on trash removal, or investigate recycling options.

A project of this sort can take a lot of class time, extending over several days or even weeks. That could be a problem in an elementary classroom where teachers are required to spend a certain amount of time on different subjects. However, because PBL is interdisciplinary, work on the project could be distributed among different subjects, such as English language arts, mathematics, science, and social studies, allowing more time for the students to work on the project and bringing coherence and meaning to their school day.

Like PBL, *problem-based learning* also refers to lessons that are based on real-world issues, so there is considerable overlap between them. We chose the term *project-based lessons* for this chapter because it places the focus on the project that students carry out rather than the problem that they are asked to solve.

STEM LESSON ESSENTIALS • Integrating Science, Technology, Engineering, and Mathematics

Also, the term *project-based* is more commonly used in reference to K–8 class-rooms. However, it bears keeping in mind that project-based lessons always begin with some interesting problem to solve, and together the qualities of project- and problem-based learning can lead to a powerful transdisciplinary experience for the students. Throughout this chapter, we'll use the acronym PBL to mean "project-based learning."

What Are the Characteristics of STEM PBL?

Well-designed PBL units have a number of characteristics that distinguish them from a typical extended classroom activity. We'll refer back to the Where Is Away? unit for examples.

- **The students are at the center of the learning process.** PBL units engage the students in open-ended, authentic tasks. These projects empower students to make decisions and apply their interests and prior learning experiences to the culminating product or performance. They are inquiry- and design-oriented and allow students some control over their decisions about how and what they will complete as their final project task. The teacher takes on the role of the "guide-by-the-side"—someone who is a facilitator and a coach. Students work in collaborative groups and assume roles that make the best use of their individual talents. Although the essential question, guidelines, and decisions on how to form project groups can be developed when planning the unit, the greatest demand on the teacher's skill will be managing the work from day to day. It will be important to allow the students to take initiative and pursue their own ideas, while at the same time providing guidance that takes into account such factors as learning objectives and safety. Finding the right balance is the key to success.
  - In the case of the Where Is Away? unit, students make many decisions related to the project, both its content (their recommendations for recycling and waste reduction) and its form (the presentations, websites, and brochures).

- **The project is central rather than peripheral to the curriculum.** Projects are selected with important learning objectives in mind, so as the students focus on the project work, they will also accomplish core learning objectives. Because learning objectives might fall into several areas of the curriculum, it will be important to introduce questions, readings, investigations, demonstrations, or other kinds of activities that help the students make progress toward answering the essential question as they develop knowledge and skills.

  - The Where Is Away? unit starts from the science objectives, including concepts of renewable and nonrenewable resources and the impact of using those resources, and also includes objectives from math, technology, engineering, language arts, and social studies. Activities for this unit include students examining the trash found in their own classrooms, interviewing school staff and outside experts, developing a cost analysis, and designing and displaying posters to encourage other students to recycle, reuse, and reduce the amount of waste they produce.

- **Projects are broken down into manageable pieces.** An effective way of doing this during the planning process, and as the work proceeds, is to think of different tiers of questions. As mentioned previously, *the essential question* launches the unit, provides a touchstone to keep everyone on track, and provides a destination for pulling ideas together at the end of the unit. *Lesson questions* are a means for helping the students break down the essential question into manageable tasks. They also provide guidance to keep the students on track, as they are tied directly to the project goals from both the students' and teacher's points of view. *Curriculum framing questions* should challenge students to connect the real-world issue that is driving the project and key concepts within the disciplines. *Content questions* are fact-based and designed to help the students move the project forward as they improve their vocabulary, gain concept knowledge, and skills.

- As noted previously, the Where Is Away? unit is broken down into smaller questions that make the material more manageable. Questions like "Where has all the trash gone in the past until now?" help integrate social studies and other disciplines into the project.

- **The project has real-world relevant connections.** Projects need to be age-appropriate and relevant to students' lives. They could involve community or outside experts who can provide supporting information and add context to the learning goals. Students should present their findings to an authentic audience, crafting and delivering a meaningful message that takes their audience's viewpoints into consideration.

  - Students in the Where Is Away? unit spend time learning about not just their school's plan for dealing with trash, but their community's waste disposal plan. The project culminates with a presentation to an authentic audience: the principal and other school staff, who may actually be able to put students' recommendations into practice.

- **The project will conclude with a product or performance.** Projects typically culminate with students demonstrating the results of their project work. This can take a number of different forms, such as a verbal presentation in front of the class or to parents or a community group; production of a model that illustrates the various design features of each group's proposed solution; written documentation of the process, evidence, recommendations; a video or Web page; or even a simulated event such as a play or a mock trial. These final products allow for student expression and ownership of learning.

  - The Where Is Away? unit gives students the opportunity to produce several different products: a website, a presentation, brochures, and posters.

- **Digital technologies support and enhance student learning.** Students should have access to a variety of digital and nondigital technologies to support their research and thinking skills and for the creation of the final products. With the help of technology, students have more control over final results and an opportunity to personalize and produce a more professional product.

- In Where Is Away? students use spreadsheets, online information sources, and word processing and other presentation tools to develop and communicate their recommendations.

- **Thinking skills are integral to project work.** Project work supports the development of both social and cognitive skills, such as teamwork, communication, and collaboration, as well as the metacognitive skills such as self-monitoring, personal reflection, and evaluation of results. These types of behaviors are the hallmark of the skills desired in today's workplace.

  - In Where Is Away? students work closely in teams, each team producing its own brochure and/or presentation. Students also receive a rubric that they use to self-assess their teamwork.

- **Instructional strategies are varied and support multiple learning styles.** To include students with various abilities, the instructional strategies should create a learning environment that promotes higher-order thinking for all students, whatever their initial level might be. Using a range of instructional strategies will help to ensure that the curricular materials are accessible to all students and provide opportunities for every student to succeed. Instruction may vary and include the use of different cooperative group strategies, graphic organizers, as well as the teacher's feedback.

  - To help accommodate the needs of all learning styles in the classroom, the teacher of the Where Is Away? unit provides a variety of small, manageable activities using a written checklist as a guide. The teacher guides students who need more support to specific prechosen websites suitable for their readability level for them to conduct their research and modifies the math assignments to include a math "buddy" to help clarify the work. English language learners could be accommodated with short oral speaking and reading roles as well as working in a blended group to help clarify their understanding. And advanced students can complete more complex spreadsheets and data analysis.

- **Projects involve ongoing and multiple types of assessment.** Clear expectations are defined and shared with the students at the beginning of a project and are revisited with multiple checks for understanding using various assessment methods. Students have models or rubrics that describe specific guidelines for what defines high-quality work and details what is expected from the beginning of the project to its conclusion. Opportunities for reflection, feedback, and adjustment are embedded within the project to ensure that students remain on track toward the final goal. (For more on assessment, see Chapter 13.)
  - Before beginning the unit, students take a preassessment to inform the teacher about their knowledge of landfills, waste management, and recycling in general, as well as their questions. The same questions can be given on a posttest. Students' products are assessed using rubrics for both content and teamwork. They also complete check sheets to assess their mathematical understanding as they work on their cost analysis.

Helpful Tips for Managing Successful PBL Experiences

As you become the guide-by-the-side, your students will begin to take on the ownership and responsibilities of their group roles. Here are a few suggestions for managing the experience:

- **Share the project goals and rubrics for judging success up front with your students.** Research has shown that highest motivation and learning occur when the teacher sets the goals but the students have latitude in deciding how they will reach the goals (Schwartz and Sadler 2007). The goals need to be clearly displayed for all to see. Help them understand and keep focused on the essential question and the learning goals and encourage them to think of the best ways to reach the goals.

- **Group your students appropriately.** Collaboration is the hallmark of PBL, but if collaboration is to take place in your classroom, the students must be shown how to work together. Groups can be assigned based on your assessment of the students' individual skills and work habits or the students can self-select their group members. The groups do not have to be together for the entire unit but can be reassigned based on needs of the task. There will also be times when you know there are fundamental skills that may need teaching or reteaching and you can group students according to the skill level to help them master the skill before they apply newly learned skills to the project work.

- **Manage the work flow for the students.** To keep the project from getting out of hand and becoming overwhelming to you and your students, set up a work schedule and make certain the students have this in the project notebook. This will help them know which tasks need to be accomplished by what date. Have check-in conferences with groups and individual students if needed.

- **Monitor the students.** Watch for content areas in which students seem to be struggling and are just being "hitchhikers" in their group. The task at hand might be too easy or too hard for some, and it might be best to stop and use "just-in-time" instruction, a quick lecture, handout, or class discussion or have them research some information to keep the work progressing.

- **Use checkpoints and milestones.** There are many ways to help accomplish this. Here are a few examples.
  - Ask the group leaders to give informal briefings on group progress.
  - Interview students and groups randomly.
  - Schedule weekly reflection time with the groups.
  - Examine progress logs of the individual students or groups.
  - Sit in with a group during their work session.
  - Conduct a debriefing session with the whole class.

STEM LESSON ESSENTIALS • Integrating Science, Technology, Engineering, and Mathematics

Celebrating class success is another hallmark of good PBL teaching. Make certain to involve parents, other classrooms, and administration in celebrating and displaying the projects or presentations. Not only is it a way for the students to feel successful but it also helps to inform others on how using this transdisciplinary teaching model helps students grow as individuals, models how they can apply their skills and knowledge in unique ways, and moves the class toward becoming successful members of their community.

Reflection

- If you are talking with a fellow colleague, how would you explain what a STEM PBL unit is all about?

- Are there times you have tried using a PBL approach and it did not seem to fit your teaching style? How would it help if you had a team to work with in developing the goals and learning outcomes for the PBL unit?

- In using cooperative learning or collaborative approaches with your students, what "tricks of the trade" have you found that help the teams work together successfully?

- Describe some ways in which you organized the work flow in a PBL unit.

- If you have not tried PBL in your classroom, were there some ideas in this chapter that might get you started planning a unit? Why or why not?

REFERENCES

Capraro, R. M., and S. W. Slough, Eds. 2009. *Project-Based Learning, An Integrated Science, Technology, Engineering, and Mathematics (STEM) Approach*. Rotterdam/Taipei: Sense Publishers.

Common Core State Standards Initiative. 2010. National Governors Association Center for Best Practices and Council of Chief State School Officers. Available at: www.corestandards .org/.

Drake, S. M., and R. C. Burns. 2004. *Meeting the Standards Through Integrated Curriculum*. Alexandria, VA: Association for Supervision and Curriculum Development.

Earth 911. "Find Local Recycling Centers." Available at: http://earth911.com/.

————. "How Plastic Gets Recycled." Video. Available at: http://earth911.com/recycling/plastic/video-how-plastic-gets -recycled/.

Environmental Protection Agency. "Municipal Solid Waste." Available at: www.epa.gov/osw/nonhaz/municipal/.

Fortus, D., J. Krajcik, R. C. Dershimerb, R. W. Marx, and R. Mamlok-Naamand. 2005. "Design-Based Science and Real-World Problem Solving." *International Journal of Science Education* 27 (7): 855–79.

Kanter, D., and S. Konstantopoulos. 2010. "The Impact of Project-Based Science on Minority Student Achievement, Attitudes, and Career Plans: An Examination of the Effects of Teacher Content Knowledge, Pedagogical Content Knowledge, and Inquiry-Based Practices." *Science Education* 94: 855–87.

Markham, T., J. Larmer, and J. Ravitz. 2003. *Project-Based Learning Handbook: A Guide to Standards-Focused Project-Based Learning for Middle and High School Teachers.* Oakland, CA: Buck Institute for Education.

McTighe, J., and G. Wiggin. 2004. *The Understanding by Design Professional Workbook.* Alexandria, VA: Association for Supervision and Curriculum Development.

National Governor's Association. 2007. "Innovate America: Building a Science, Technology, Engineering and Math Agenda." Available at: www.nga.org/files/live/sites/NGA/files/pdf/0702INNOVATIONSTEM.PDF.

Satchwell, R., and R. L. Loepp. 2002. "Designing and Implementing an Integrated Math, Science, and Technology Curriculum for the Middle School." *Journal of Industrial Teacher Education.* Spring. Available at: http://scholar.lib.vt.edu/ejournals/JITE/v39n3/satchwell.html. Accessed November 9, 2010.

Schwartz, M. S., and P. M. Sadler. 2007. "Empowerment in Science Curriculum Development: A Microdevelopmental Approach." *International Journal of Science Education* 8 (18): 987–1017.

SEPUP. 2003. *Waste Disposal: Computers and the Environment.* Ronkonkoma, NY: Lab-Aids, Inc.

Tomlinson, C. A., and J. McTighe. 2006. *Integrating Differentiated Instruction and Understanding by Design.* Alexandria, VA: Association for Supervision and Curriculum Development.

CHAPTER 13

STEM Assessment

Assessment is an ongoing process aimed at understanding and improving student learning. For it involves making our expectations explicit and public; setting appropriate criteria and high standards for learning quality; systematically gathering, analyzing, and interpreting evidence to determine how well performance matches those expectations and standards; and using the resulting information to document, explain, and improve performance.

—"Reassessing (and Defining) Assessment," T. A. Angelo (1995, 2)

This chapter was written by author Jo Anne Vasquez and is deeply rooted in her own early experiences with assessment and how her understanding of assessment evolved over the years.

BEFORE READING THIS CHAPTER,

think about your own attitudes about assessment. How do you define assessment? How does it interact with the way you teach and how you adjust your teaching to best meet your students' needs?

A New Vision of Assessment

Many, many years ago when I began my education career as an elementary teacher, I remember well that instructional planning was divided into three components, which were approached as three separate, sequential steps. We had curriculum, instruction, and assessment. Assessment was the finish line. It was where we wanted the students to aspire to, the level we wanted them to reach at the end of their learning journey. Believe it or not, we really didn't know or think much about what was happening along the way.

As educators became seriously concerned that our students were not reaching higher levels of achievement, things began to change. When state and national standards began to enter the equation, the spotlight shifted, and it soon became clear that the three areas—curriculum, assessment, and instruction—were closely interrelated. They informed and reinforced each other. As a consequence of that realization, as a profession we have moved away from viewing assessment as the end goal or finish line for our students. Good assessment strategies help to inform not only how our students are learning, but also help how we are teaching and how to adjust and monitor our instruction to meet the needs of all our students. We have also realized that assessment is not only the teacher's domain. Our students also need data on their own performance and how to move from where they are to where they need to be.

Assessment is a wide and complex system of strategies, techniques, and methods supported by a large body of research. So we will not attempt to cover it all. Instead, this chapter will present a few broad ideas about assessment and focus on the process of assessment through the lens of a STEM teacher.

Two Frameworks for Assessment

In Chapter 2 we discussed the 1999 National Research Council report, *How People Learn* (Bransford et al. 1999, 121–22), which summarized the results of thirty years of research on learning and teaching. A good learning environment for our students needs to be *knowledge-centered*, based on what we want students to know and be able to do as a result of the learning experience; *learner-centered*, connecting the strengths, interests, and preconceptions of learners to their current academic tasks and learning goals and helping students learn about themselves as learners; and *assessment-centered*, providing multiple opportunities to monitor and make visible students' progress in revising their thinking and applying their growing knowledge to new situations and tasks. A learning environment that weaves together these three strands creates a fabric of educational experiences in a holistic process rather than being delivered as separate fibers during instruction. This is especially true for STEM teaching.

In Chapter 8, we briefly described the backward design process, which starts with standards and assessment. (We'll discuss it more in the next chapter.) Starting with what we want our students to know and be able to do and deciding what evidence will demonstrate their progress helps to focus on the important questions: Did the students learn it? How do I know? How deep is their knowledge, and how well can they apply it? How might I adjust my teaching to be more effective for learners with different needs (Tomlinson and McTighe 2006)?

These two frameworks have helped me break out of my earlier and more limited vision of assessment as something that I had to do after I was done teaching and toward seeing assessment as an essential part of what I did in the classroom every day to help my students learn. These ideas will weave throughout the rest of this chapter, providing the underpinnings of the specific strategies that we describe.

Interdisciplinary Assessment

Assessment strategies used in the disciplines can also be used for interdisciplinary teaching. That is because integrated units are built on standards and learning objectives from the disciplines. Consider, for example, the Giants and Borrowers unit from Chapter 11. To measure success, the teacher would use assessment criteria that are similar to any class on ratio and proportion. For example:

- Were the students repeatedly using algorithms to calculate the dimensions for the furniture or did they exhibit some flexibility and dexterity in understanding number relationships when converting their measurements?
- Could the students describe how they arrived at a calculated measurement or defend their measurement when questioned by a peer?
- As the students generated their data, were they accurate in their measurements and did they make effective use of the appropriate tools available for the level of difficulty in the task?

In addition to assessing disciplinary knowledge, however, most integrated STEM units also include important learning objectives that cut across the disciplines. For example, communication skills do not fall only within the realm of English language arts, as they are integral to every subject. Cooperation, teamwork, and problem solving are not found just in one subject but cut across all disciplines. The students need to have an understanding of the content (knowing) but must also be able to show what they know by being able to apply it (the doing).

The idea that assessing STEM learning involves the same strategies used for assessing disciplinary knowledge and skills and for assessing broader capabilities that cut across the disciplines is the central organizing idea of this chapter.

The Purposes of Assessment

Following is a list of tools commonly used for assessment within the disciplines. What makes them *interdisciplinary* assessment tools is how they are used.

- checklists
- rubrics
- classroom tests
- maps
- self-assessments
- peer assessments
- graphic organizers
- concept maps
- portfolios
- conferences

Each of these tools can be used for summative, diagnostic, or formative purposes.

Summative assessments determine what students have learned at the conclusion of an instructional unit or segment. These assessments tend to be evaluative, and teachers mostly use them to report assessment results as a

STEM LESSON ESSENTIALS • Integrating Science, Technology, Engineering, and Mathematics

score or grade. Familiar examples of summative assessment tools include tests, performance tasks, final exams, culminating projects, and work portfolios.

Diagnostic assessment, also known as *preassessment*, typically precedes instruction. Teachers may use this type of assessment to check the students' prior knowledge and skill levels to help plan the instructional unit or to group students so that those with greater knowledge and skills can help the other students. This use of assessment tools is especially helpful with the interdisciplinary approach because it is necessary to know what the students are capable of doing and understanding before proceeding with teaching. If you have a lesson that requires the students to apply rates of change or calculate speed, then it is best to find out if the students are familiar with the mathematical procedures necessary for success before starting the activity. Otherwise the students may become discouraged or disruptive.

Formative assessments occur concurrently with instruction. These are the ongoing monitoring activities that provide specific feedback to teachers and students for the purpose of guiding the instruction and improving the learning experience. Sometimes called *classroom assessments*, these can include both formal methods, such as quizzes, student-constructed concept maps, learning logs, and portfolio reviews, as well as informal methods such as asking questions to stimulate discussion, observations of small group work, and asking your students to talk about their thinking as they work on a problem.

Assessment and Grading Practices

Keeping these three types of assessments in mind, Jay McTighe and Ken O'Connor (2005) have framed seven assessment and grading practices that we think are especially helpful for effective STEM units.

1. **Use summative assessment tasks to frame meaningful performance goals for students.** Presenting authentic performance tasks at the *beginning* of a new unit provides a meaningful vision of the targeted learning goals for the students. An authentic assessment task does not simply

require recall of facts but rather the application of knowledge applied to new situations so as to reveal deep understanding and skills. The sooner the students understand what will be required of them at the conclusion of the unit, the easier it will be for them to learn the required concepts and skills.

2. **Show criteria and models in advance.** Presenting the criteria for success and modeling examples at the beginning of the unit help students understand not only what they are asked to do but also what different levels of performance look like. Rubrics are widely used for this purpose. A rubric is a chart listing the different categories or criteria for judging success and levels of achievement for each category. Examples of rubrics are given at the end of this chapter.

3. **Assess before teaching.** Diagnostic assessments are important at the outset of a unit. These will give the teacher clear indicators of students' skill levels and uncover any existing misconceptions. By revealing these at the onset of the project, the teacher can include opportunities to teach those skills and concepts necessary for success with all students, as well as providing additional assistance to a subset of students who may need targeted instruction to complete the task.

4. **Offer appropriate choices.** When planning a culminating assessment, it is helpful if the students have a choice in how they will demonstrate what they have learned. Options might include a presentation, project, display, notebook, or portfolio. This strategy has the advantage of allowing students to rely on their strengths and to demonstrate learning that the students consider most important. However, when giving students choices, it is also important to provide a common rubric to establish the criteria for judging success.

5. **Provide feedback early and often.** Feedback is the key ingredient for student success. This feedback must meet four criteria: It must be timely, specific, understandable to the receiver, and designed to allow for self-adjustment on the student's part (Wiggins 1998).

STEM LESSON ESSENTIALS • Integrating Science, Technology, Engineering, and Mathematics

6. **Encourage self-assessment and goal setting.** As teachers we know that setting goals for ourselves helps provide a clear path for us to follow. The same holds true for students. The most effective learners set their learning goals, employ proven strategies, monitor, and self-assess their work. Rubrics can help the students here as well. They can help students become more effective at honest self-appraisal and establish a path for self-improvement.

7. **Allow new evidence of achievement to replace old evidence.** Classroom assessments need to focus on how well, not when, the students have mastered the designated knowledge or skill.

These seven assessment strategies are broad but help us to clearly lay out the types of assessments that can be used in our classroom, especially for STEM teaching and learning. STEM is not some foreign type of learning that needs to have different assessment strategies from what you normally use, but it does present an opportunity to engage students in demonstrating their understanding in a variety of different ways.

These practices are consistent with a recommendation by Marzano (1992) that students are most likely to put forth the required effort when there is: (1) task clarity, (2) relevance, and (3) a high potential for success.

Assessing Project-Based Learning

Project-based learning (PBL), as described in Chapter 12, takes students and teachers away from traditional paper-and-pencil tests and moves them toward authentic assessment practices because teachers are no longer teaching just the content. The instructional goals associated with PBL are tied to the application of the knowledge and skills that students employ as they go about developing their project. This calls for a variety of performance assessments of the disciplinary content, higher-order thinking skills, and quality of the results.

Tests, written reports, and traditional research papers or essays can be used in PBL units. However, assessment strategies must also include ways to capture the process-oriented outcomes of PBL. Often the products from a project are designed to accomplish both goals—to measure students' content knowledge and skills as well as how these are deployed in a real-world context. To use these products for assessment, it is very helpful to develop a rubric.

The process of writing a rubric requires thinking deeply about what we want the students to know and be able to demonstrate through the learning experience. A rubric can clearly differentiate levels of student performance and when written well can provide a clear description of what is expected. Rubrics are never meant to be a mystery to the students. Knowing in advance how success will be measured will give students a much greater sense of fairness, help them to be fully engaged in the outcomes of the work, and encourage teams to be more inclusive so students with a range of ability levels can become functional and contributing team members.

To be effective, rubrics should have the following elements:

Impact of performance: Describes a successful performance. Gives the purposes, goals, and desired results expected from the team members.

Work quality and craftsmanship: Defines the overall polish, organization, and rigor of the work so that greater degrees of effort can be rewarded.

Adequacy of methods and behaviors: Describes how the quality of the procedures and manner of presentation, both prior to and during performance, will be evaluated.

Validity of content: Defines the expectations for the accuracy of the ideas, skills, or materials used and delineates the varying levels of rigor.

Sophistication of knowledge: Provides ideas and guidelines to encourage students to improve the complexity or maturity of the knowledge displayed.

Figure 13.1 is a sample rubric that has been designed for use with a task in the PBL unit, Where Is Away? (described in Chapter 12). The main outcome was to do presentations to other classrooms or to the school administration to talk about their findings and give ideas for conservation and recycling. In developing their presentations, each team of students was asked to develop a script for a particular grade level or a poster or other means to communicate the most important messages from their study. The rubric in Figure 13.1 was developed to assess the quality of these final products. It was given to the teams before they started to develop their messages, so they would understand how their work would be assessed.

In Figure 13.1, notice that the levels of achievement written in each cell are briefly stated and are assumed to include lower level accomplishments as well. For example, next to "Writing Style and Purpose," level 4 performance states "All elements are present to convey the message and make it meaningful." This statement implies inclusion of the level 3 performance that "data are used in the message."

Assessing Team Participation

When the rubric for assessing the quality of the team's products was first presented to the students, they were told that each team member was expected to contribute to the final product and that the assessment of the product would apply equally to all of the team members. Although that approach usually encourages peer pressure to get all students to participate fully, it does not help to assess how each individual on the team develops teamwork skills. The rubric for self-assessment of teamwork skills in Figure 13.2 was developed for that purpose.

It is important to point out that the importance of teamwork is not just emphasized at the beginning and end of the unit. Rather, the students need to frequently reflect on their teamwork skills. The students are required to keep student notebooks and to frequently assess how they feel they are doing and to reflect on how their team as a whole is functioning. The notebooks provide an opportunity for the teacher to assess progress and to intervene when necessary to help the teams operate smoothly.

Finally, it is important not to overemphasize the role of assessment in building teamwork skills. The most important work of the teacher is to establish a community of respect and cooperation in the classroom. The students will be

Figure 13.1 Rubric for final product.

Category	4	3	2	1	Points
Writing style and purpose	All elements are present to convey the message and make it meaningful. Past and present waste and recycling are represented. There is a meaningful call to action on the part of the listener and the reader.	Data is used in the message. Some historical background is presented but lacks detail. Information is presented to encourage a call to action on part of the listener and the reader.	Data is used but not conveyed clearly. The material is presented in a way that does not encourage the reader or listener to become involved.	Little or no data is used or is not accurate. The poster is not appealing and does not provide a call to action. The script is not persuasive and lacks most of the information that has been gathered by the class.	
Writing and vocabulary	There are zero mistakes with grammar, usage, or spelling. Technical language is used and defined. The message is clear and persuasive.	The poster or brochure has 2 to 3 grammar, usage, and/or spelling mistakes. The new words are defined for the listener and the reader of the poster.	The poster or brochure has 4 or 5 grammar usage or spelling mistakes. New vocabulary is introduced but not used in context so that the reader or listener will understand the meaning.	There are more than 6 grammar, usage, or spelling mistakes and no new vocabulary is introduced.	
Visual appeal and graphic design of the poster and brochure	The poster and brochure are eye catching and easy to read. Text and graphics create a balance to the message. Information is well organized for the reader.	The poster and brochure are attractive and well organized with the information. The text and graphics are not well balanced but they do convey the message.	The information is organized but it is difficult to read and hard to understand. Graphics are used but do not effectively convey the message well enough to be persuasive to the reader or keep his or her attention.	Formatting and organization of the poster and brochure are confusing to the reader. Graphics are not used effectively and the message is lost to the reader.	
Team grade-level script and presentation	The content of the script is well organized using language that is appropriate for the grade level. The message is clear and provides a call to action.	The content of the script is organized so it is easy to follow the message. The presentation shows some persuasion and a call to action.	The content of the script is organized for the most part but the flow of the message is unclear. The presentation is not persuasive. No call to action is presented.	No clear logical organization structure around the script and messaging. The script is not appropriate for the grade level the team was assigned to engage.	

Figure 13.2 Rubric for self-assessment of teamwork skills.

Criteria	Performance Levels				Student	Teacher
	4	**3**	**2**	**1**		
Cooperation (Cite an example)	I work well with all group members and I share the workload equally.	I work well with most of the group but at times I do not share the workload.	I work well with the group some of the time but the other group members do most of the work.	I do not work well with the group and I do not partici-pate in sharing the workload.		
Participation (Cite an example)	I participate fully and am always on task in the group and class.	I participate most of the time and am often on task.	I do participate but also find that I waste time a lot and have a hard time staying on task.	I do not par-ticipate with my group and most of the time I am not on task.		
Listening (Cite an example)	I am attentive and listen to what my teammates have to say before I speak or ask questions.	I listen most of the time and I try to pay attention to what my team-mates are saying.	I listen some of the time but I'm anxious to share with my group what I know, therefore I tend to interrupt.	I don't pay much attention to what my teammates are saying as I have my own ideas that I want to get heard.		
Feedback (Cite an cxamplc)	I give constructive feedback most of thc timc.	I give constructive feedback often.	I only give feed-back when I am asked directly.	I never give feedback to my teammates.		
Leadership (Cite an example)	I welcome the opportunity to take a leadership role and help others in my group participate.	Most of the time I'm open to taking on a leadership role.	I can take a leadership role but would rather do it myself.	Most of the time I prefer to be just a group member and not be in a leadership role.		
Work Habits (Cite an example)	I am always on task and never need reminders to do the work. I encourage my group members to do the same.	Most of the time I am on task and seldom need to be reminded to do the work and participate.	There have been several times when I've had to be reminded by the team to stay on task.	I try but need to be reminded to stay on task and participate with my team.		

heavily dependent on one another as they work together giving constructive feedback, asking for clarification, celebrating each other's victories, and supporting one another's efforts. This breaks down the competitive walls between students and allows for cooperative and successful student teams where all can share in the rewards.

Everyday Assessment in the Science Classroom

We close this chapter with a comment that the best teaching occurs when assessment and instruction are so closely joined that it is impossible to distinguish one from the other. Our coauthor Cary Sneider was a contributing author to the book *Everyday Assessment in the Science Classroom* (Atkin and Coffey 2003). In his chapter, "Examining Students' Work," he posed the question, "Assessment or Instruction?" where he related the following experience about working at the Museum of Science in Boston.

> One of the Museum's presenters of live programs introduces a large snake to the audience and asks, "How much of this snake is tail, and how much is body?" To encourage visitors to think more deeply about this the presenter added the information that some people think that a snake is all body, others think it is all tail. The presenter allows time for the visitors to respond and leads them in a lively discussion about the snake. To help the visitors realize that in fact they already have the knowledge they need to agree on an answer he asks them to picture a dog or cat, and to think about what else they find where the tail meets the body. A few begin to giggle, and the instructor points out quite seriously that excretion is essential for all living things. At that point he invites a brave member of the audience up to see if the snake has a place to excrete waste, which in snakes is called a "vent." That resolves the discussion, and the visitors leave understanding that snakes do indeed have a tail, and they understood why all along. (Sneider 2003)

You will recognize that this teaching style is the Socratic questioning approach. Cary noted that "Socrates may have been the first person in history to advocate using questions to assess students' understanding as a means for instruction."

STEM LESSON ESSENTIALS • Integrating Science, Technology, Engineering, and Mathematics

What struck me as I read this account is how every question we pose to students opens a door into their thinking. By asking more open-ended, thought-provoking questions, we can open even more doors. Assessment extends even further to gathering and analyzing students' artifacts and observing collaborative group behaviors. All of these inputs give us new insights into evaluating not only our students' thinking but our own teaching methods as well. Assessment and instruction as well as curriculum are all joined together and we cannot, nor should we, separate the three of them.

Reflection

- How have your views on assessment evolved during your teaching career?

- Think of your own assessment habits. Which of the tools listed do you use? Which ones are new to you? How might you make use of a different tool for your next assessment task?

- Do you use assessment for all three purposes discussed in this chapter: diagnostic, formative, and summative? If not do you plan to use assessment in different ways in the future?

- When creating your own rubric, do you incorporate all of the elements as suggested? How might you adapt your current rubric to accommodate more of these elements?

REFERENCES

Atkin, J. M., and J. E. Coffey, Eds. 2003. *Everyday Assessment in the Science Classroom.* Arlington, VA: National Science Teachers Association.

Angelo, T. A. 1995. "Reassessing (and Defining) Assessment." *AAHE Bulletin* 48 (2): 7–9.

Brandsford, J. D., A. L. Brown, and R. R. Cocking, Eds. 1999. *How People Learn: Brain, Mind, Experience and School.* Washington, DC: National Research Council. Available at: www.nap.edu/catalog/9853.html.

Brookhart, S. M. 2010. *How to Assess Higher-Order Thinking Skills in Your Classroom.* Alexandria, VA: ASCD.

Drake, S. M. 2007. *Creating Standards-Based Integrated Curriculum.* 2d ed. Thousand Oaks, CA: Corwin Press.

Intel's K–12 Education website. Available at: www.intel.com/education/k12.

Marzano, R. 1992. *A Different Kind of Classroom: Teaching with Dimensions of Learning.* Alexandria, VA: ASCD.

McTighe, J., and K. O'Connor. 2005. "Seven Practices for Effective Learning." ASCD, *Educational Leadership* 63 (3): 10–17.

Sneider, C. 2003. "Examining Students' Work." In *Everyday Assessment in the Science Classroom*, edited by J. M. Atkin and J. E. Coffey. Arlington, VA: National Science Teachers Association.

Stiggins, R. J. 1997. *Student-Centered Classroom Assessment.* Upper Saddle River, NJ: Prentice-Hall, Inc.

Tomlinson, C. A., and J. McTighe. 2006. *Integrating & Differentiated Instruction, Understanding by Design.* Alexandria, VA: ASCD.

14

Getting Started on Your STEM Teaching

As the title suggests this book is about good design—of curriculum, assessment, and instruction—focused on developing and deepening understanding of important ideas. Posed as a question, considered throughout the book and from many perspectives, the essence of this book is this: How do we make it more likely—by our design—that more students really understand what they are asked to learn? *So often, by contrast, those who "get it" are learners who come to us already able and articulate—understanding by good fortune. What must our planning entail to have an intellectual impact on everyone: the less experienced; the highly able, but unmotivated; the less able; those with varied interests and styles?*

—*Learning and Design, Expanded 2nd ed.*, Wiggins and McTighe (2005, 3–4)

BEFORE READING THIS CHAPTER, reflect on the methods that you already use to plan instruction. Do you use the "backward design" method proposed by Wiggins and McTighe or some other approach? What do you like about the approach you now use? What would you like to change?

Backward Design

At its core, teaching is an art that calls on its practitioners to work simultaneously in multiple media, with multiple elements. Central to our STEM teaching journey is *what* we ought to teach and what we want our students to *know*, *understand*, and *be able to do*. Coherent, meaning-rich curriculum provides opportunities for the learning process to happen *within* students, not *to* them. Providing STEM learning experiences will begin with the *big ideas* and *essential questions* to help all students understand the content in the standards. To that end, we have adapted the three-stage backward design process for curriculum planning (McTighe and Wiggins 2004; Wiggins and McTighe 2005). Although we recommend reading the complete books written by Grant Wiggins and Jay McTighe, this brief chapter will get you started if you're not already familiar with their work.

Backward planning asks educators to consider the following three stages in planning:

- **Identify desired results.** What should students know, understand, and be able to do? What content is worthy of understanding? What "enduring understandings" do you want them to gain from your classes? What "essential questions" do you want your students to explore?
- **Determine acceptable evidence for assessment.** How will you know whether your students have achieved the desired results? What will you accept as evidence of student understanding and proficiency?
- **Plan learning experiences.** What prior knowledge and skills will your students need to perform effectively and achieve the desired results? What activities can be used to foster integration? What levels of integration will be most effective to accomplish the learning goals? How will the lessons be sequenced? Is there an opportunity for the students to participate in a transdisciplinary experience? How can you plan for such an experience? What resources and materials will you need to accomplish your goals?

Backward planning provides a coherent way of thinking about what we really want students to know and understand. Often, lessons or activities are fun and engaging, but unless they have a purpose or a goal they are unlikely to have a long-term impact. STEM requires creative thinking, planning, and most of all coordination of curricular strategies that will give your students rich and meaningful learning experiences.

If you already have a favorite planning template, then by all means use it. If not, we suggest the template in Figure 14.1 that you can use to get started planning effective STEM lessons.

Figure 14.1 Planning template for a STEM lesson or unit.

A. Identify Desired Results

Strategy 1: Identify the content standards.

- What are the content standards and twenty-first-century skills that this lesson/unit will teach?

Strategy 2: Identify big ideas and key concepts.

- What are the "big ideas," key concepts, knowledge, and skills that describe what students will know and be able to do?

Strategy 3: Identify the essential question(s).

- What intriguing questions will elevate the students' thinking, foster inquiry, and build conceptual understandings?

Strategy 4: Establish what the students will know and be able to do as a result of this unit or lesson.

- What prior knowledge and skills do the students need to understand the content?

- What new knowledge and skills will students acquire from these activities?

- What should they be able to do as a result of such knowledge and skills?

B. Determine Acceptable Evidence for Assessment

Strategy 5: Create multiple and ongoing assessment opportunities throughout the learning experiences.

- What formative assessments will be used to measure progress toward students' understanding and inform instruction?

- What criteria are needed for the students to demonstrate understanding of the standards across different integrated content subjects?

- Where appropriate how can rubrics be used to measure student performance?

- How will students think about their ideas and assess their own progress?

- What other assessment methods will be used to help students demonstrate their understanding (tests, quizzes, observations, homework, presentations, journals)?

(Continues)

Figure 14.1 Planning template for a STEM lesson or unit. *(Continued)*

C. Plan Learning Experiences

Strategy 6: Design interdisciplinary learning activities.

- Which of the three integrated STEM approaches will be the most effective goals?

- What learning experiences will enable the students to understand the concepts and skills?

- Which STEM practices should students be engaged in?

- How will the learning experiences be constructed to provide for relevance and real-world experiences for the students?

- What Guiding Principles does the developing plan reflect?

- How can I tailor instruction to my students who may have special needs, interests, and abilities?

An Example of Using the Planning Template

In this section, author Cary Sneider shares how he used the template to help develop the unit in Chapter 6, Gearing Up to Teach STEM Practices. The target audience is fourth-grade students.

A. Identify Desired Results

Strategy 1 starts by identifying the content standards relevant to the unit. If you already have a curriculum, this may already be done for you; but if you are developing one from scratch, as I did in this case, it's important to identify the relevant standards. At this writing the best source is *A Framework for K–12 Science Education: Practices, Crosscutting Concepts, and Core Ideas* (National Research Council [NRC] 2012), because it includes a rich description of what students are expected to learn in three of the STEM fields and it is aligned with the Common Core State Standards in mathematics. The statements in the *Framework* are referred to as "endpoints," meaning they describe what students need to learn by the end of a grade band. Eventually these statements will be transformed into specific performance standards in the *Next Generation Science Standards*. For now, however, the following statements from the *Framework* are the best we

STEM LESSON ESSENTIALS • Integrating Science, Technology, Engineering, and Mathematics

have. Each refers to what students should know and be able to do by the end of fifth grade.

Technology: Over time, people's needs and wants change, as do their demands for new and improved technologies. Engineers improve existing technologies or develop new ones to increase their benefits and decrease known risks to meet societal demands (NRC 2012, 213).

Science: Each force acts on one particular object and has both a strength and a direction (NRC 2012, 115). Objects in contact exert forces on each other (friction, elastic pushes and pulls) (117). Energy can be moved from place to place by moving objects or through sound, light, or electric currents (122).

Mathematics: Explain why a fraction a/b is equivalent to a fraction $(n \times a)/(n \times b)$ by using visual fraction models, with attention to how the number and size of the parts differ even though the two fractions themselves are the same size. Use this principle to recognize and generate equivalent fractions (Common Core State Standards, Mathematics, grade 4).

Engineering: Possible solutions to a problem are limited by available materials and resources (constraints). The success of a designed solution is determined by considering the desired features of a solution (criteria). Different proposals for solutions can be compared on the basis of how well each one meets the specified criteria for success or how well each takes the constraints into account (NRC 2012, 205).

Strategy 2 is a process of choosing the "big ideas" that you want students to learn. In this case, I decided that the mathematics would be the most important focus for this unit, because fractions are challenging for many fourth-grade students; and especially the idea of equivalent fractions that they are expected to master at the fourth-grade level. However, the other STEM fields would play important supporting roles. An engaging engineering project would provide the motivation and opportunity for the students to apply what they were learning. The unit would also provide opportunities for me to help the students clarify the distinction between force and energy, which are important concepts that students frequently confuse with each other. The technology statement from the *Framework* would provide an excellent Internet research assignment as there are many sites that explain how people's changing needs resulted in improvements in the form, materials, size, and precision of gear technologies.

Strategy 3 is to identify essential questions that target higher-level thinking skills (comparison, synthesis, analysis, evaluation, creation), ensure student activities are compelling and engaging, and place the focus on important topics. Not all the questions on the worksheet that I developed for the unit (Figure 14.2) are essential, but they are useful to get the students to focus on the important things as they explore the gears. Which of the questions do you think meet the description of "essential questions"?

Strategy 4 takes into account what you expect students to already understand and what new knowledge you expect them to gain. For example, by fourth grade in science students are expected to know that forces are pushes and pulls. The new learning is to realize that energy of motion can be transferred from one place to another through forces. In mathematics students are expected to be familiar with fractions and even equivalent fractions in simple cases. The new learning is to recognize where the concept of equivalent fractions can be applied in the real world—as, for example, when they realize that gears with teeth in the ratio 8:16 have turning ratios of 1:2.

B. Determine Acceptable Evidence for Assessment

Strategy 5 is creating multiple and ongoing assessment opportunities throughout the learning experiences. The worksheet provides the primary vehicle for generating such evidence. But rather than just taking the worksheets home for grading after class, I found the most effective use of the worksheets for assessment to be listening to groups of students in class as they attempted to answer the questions on the worksheets. In many cases, I was able to make suggestions to help them try different approaches or ask further guiding questions to help them answer the questions. The evidence of successful learning included not

Figure 14.2 Worksheet for Gearing Up unit—page 1.

Gear Technology

The goal of this activity is for you to become familiar with gear technology. Play with the gears, see how they fit together, and make sketches to answer the following questions.

1. How can you get one gear to turn another gear in the *opposite* direction?

2. How can you get one gear to turn another gear in the *same* direction?

3. If you have three meshed gears and the first one turns clockwise, which way does the third gear turn?

4. How can you turn a gear once and make another gear turn *twice*?

5. S-T-R-E-T-C-H your mind! If you have 101 meshed gears and the first one turns clockwise, which way does the 101st gear turn?

Gear Science

Play with the gears for a few minutes then answer the following questions.

1. When you put two gears together and turn one, does it push or pull the other gear? How do you know?

2. How could you use gears and a piece of string to lift a paper clip without touching it?

3. How do gears transfer energy from one place to another?

(Continues)

Figure 14.2 Worksheet for Gearing Up unit—page 2. *(Continued)*

Gear Math

Use the sticky dots and gears to help you answer the following questions.

1. Find a pair of gears so that if you turn one gear twice, the other gear will turn once. How many teeth are there on each of the two gears?

   _____ Teeth and _____ Teeth

2. Find a pair of gears so that if you turn one of the gears three times the other gear will turn twice. How many teeth are there on each of the two gears?

   _____ Teeth and _____ Teeth

3. How can you represent the data you have collected?

4. What did you discover?

5. S-T-R-E-T-C-H your mind! Choose a different pair of gears. Predict how many times the second gear will turn if the first gear turns once, twice, or three times. Explain how you made your prediction.

Gear Engineering

Next week is the start of the holiday shopping season, and your boss would like you to create a window display that will capture the attention of shoppers. She hands you several figurines of angels and a box of toy gears and she says she wants you to create an eye-catching moving display. When you ask her to say more about what she wants you to do, she just says, "Use your imagination! Just make it great!"

STEM LESSON ESSENTIALS • Integrating Science, Technology, Engineering, and Mathematics

only the answers that each student wrote on their worksheets, but also the discussions among the students that revealed their current understanding and how that understanding changed as they talked with each other and built structures with the gears.

C. Plan Learning Experiences

Strategy 6 is to design the interdisciplinary learning activities that would provide the evidence of learning and address the standards described above. I have come to realize that the process of designing learning experiences is very similar to the engineering design process described in the NRC's *Framework*. Just as an engineering design project begins by defining the problem to be solved and criteria for success, developing a learning experience begins by defining the standards to be addressed and the evidence that students have learned. The activity is a solution to the problem. Like most engineered solutions, the initial idea is almost never the final answer. Rather, there is a process of testing, revising, testing again, and sometimes even going back to redefine the problem.

In the case of the gears activity, redefining the problem involved going back and reconsidering whether or not the standards "fit together" as an interdisciplinary unit. The original plan was to develop a presentation for a National Science Teachers Association conference illustrating an elementary-level STEM unit that focused on the connection between mathematics and science. The big idea of equivalent fractions and ratios in mathematics seemed to be a natural connection to science, and evidence for understanding would naturally be students' abilities to apply their mathematical concepts and skills to a physical device. That led to the idea of gears, commonly taught in science in a unit on simple machines (a combination of a wheel and axle and a lever). The initial decision to use gears suggested the idea of forces and transfer of energy. A search of the *Framework* revealed some excellent connections at the appropriate grade level. Fitting engineering into the lesson involved a Web search for activities related to gears, which turned up a website by Children's Engineering Educators, LLC, which yielded the engineering activity on page 2 of the worksheet.[1] That effort led, in turn, to the engineering and technology goals described here.

Like all engineering projects, designing an integrative STEM unit also involves consideration of constraints. The first time I presented this activity I had just thirty minutes for the participants to do the activities, discuss their findings, and then reflect on how the unit integrates STEM. Although it was rushed, I did gather some evidence that the participants saw the connection between science and mathematics. Listening to small groups discussing the activities led to the two "S-T-R-E-T-C-H" activities that encouraged higher-order thinking, which I added to the worksheet, that greatly enriched the activity when I had two hours to present the activity and lead participants in a discussion of the meaning of the four STEM literacies (discussed in Chapter 2), the guiding principles of integrated STEM teaching (Chapter 3), and the STEM practices (Chapter 5).

In other words, developing integrative STEM units is not a linear process. It is an iterative engineering process, which involves defining the problem, generating and testing solutions, revisiting the problem to be solved, then further testing and refinement of the instructional activities and assessments, until it reaches your instructional goals.

Reflection

- Think of your own lesson planning habits. Do you take into consideration the ultimate goal of the instruction as the first step in planning?

- How does the "backward mapping" model impact how you now think about your lesson planning? Describe a lesson you planned that would fit this model.

- Which of the three stages would you find easiest to include in lesson planning? Which one is hardest? How might the planning template make the more difficult stages easier to implement?

---

[1]Gears 1, 2, and 3. Available at: www.galaxy.net/~k12/machines/.

REFERENCES

Banilower, E., K. Cohen, J. Pasley, and I. Weiss. 2008. *Effective Science Instruction: What Does Research Tell Us?* Portsmouth, NH: RMC Research Corporation.

Common Core State Standards Initiative. Mathematics. 2010. National Governors Association Center for Best Practices and Council of Chief State School Officers. Available at: www.corestandards.org/.

Marzano, R., and D. Pickering. 2001. *Classroom Instruction That Works: Research-Based Strategies for Increasing Student Achievement.* Alexandria, VA: Association for Supervision and Curriculum Development.

McTighe, J., and G. Wiggins. 2004. *Understanding by Design Professional Development Workbook.* Alexandria, VA: Association for Supervision and Curriculum.

Mid-continent Research for Education and Learning (McREL). 2005. *A Participant's Manual for Classroom Instruction That Works.* Aurora, CO: McREL.

National Research Council. 2012. *A Framework for K–12 Science Education: Practices, Crosscutting Concepts, and Core Ideas.* Committee on a Conceptual Framework for New K–12 Science Education Standards. Board on Science Education, Division of Behavioral and Social Sciences and Education. Washington, DC: The National Academy Press. Available online at: www.nap.edu/catalog.php?record_id=13165.

Tomlinson, C. A., and J. McTighe. 2006. *Integrating Differentiated Instruction + Understanding by Design.* Alexandria, VA: Association for Supervision and Curriculum.

Tweed, A. 2009. *Designing Effective Science Instruction.* Arlington, VA: National Science Teachers Association.

Wiggins, G., and J. McTighe. 2005. *Learning and Design, Expanded 2nd ed.* Alexandria, VA: Association for Supervision and Curriculum Development.

15

Implementing STEM in a Middle School

This chapter was written by Jake Prokop, a District Resource Teacher.

BEFORE READING THIS CHAPTER

about interdisciplinary teaching at Buchanan Middle School in Tampa, Florida, reflect on times that you've had students read a story and think about its implications for our lives today. *Frankenstein*, the story that is featured in this chapter about reaching across the middle school curriculum, is especially relevant in light of today's technologies for engineering new life-forms.

Considerations of the historical, social, cultural, and ethical aspects of science and its applications, as well as of engineering and the technologies it develops, need a place in the natural science curriculum and classroom [32, 33]. The framework is designed to help students develop an understanding not only that the various disciplines of science and engineering are interrelated but also that they are human endeavors. As such, they may raise issues that are not solved by scientific and engineering methods alone.

—A Framework for K–12 Science Education: Practices, Crosscutting Concepts, and Core Ideas (National Research Council 2012, 8)

Welcome to Buchanan Middle School

Buchanan Middle School is an average grade 6–8 school with diverse demographics. The STEM Institute is a small school within the walls of Buchanan Middle School, based on the "Career Academy" model. It is one of eight STEM Institutes in the district, each with a different theme, such as engineering, premedical, maritime, or environmental resources. The theme of the STEM Institute at Buchanan is biotechnology. Because students can earn high school credit for some of the eighth-grade courses at the STEM Institute, students must first apply and meet high academic performance standards on the Florida Comprehensive Achievement Test.

All of the teachers at the STEM Institute work together and teach the entire cohort of sixth to eighth graders. Students have the same teachers for all three years while participating in the program. The teachers have a common planning time and common lunch time to allow for developing coordinated curriculum plans. Because the STEM Institute's theme is bioengineering, the teachers infuse or "flavor" the curriculum with topics relevant to biology and engineering. Over time the teachers have naturally evolved programs that embody the five guiding principles outlined in Chapter 3. They integrate courses with the common theme of biotechnology; establish relevance by frequently noting the real-world applications of biotechnology; emphasize twenty-first-century skills by providing opportunities for students to work together on creative projects; challenge the students with engaging activities that require higher-level thinking; and mix it up by providing a variety of ways for students to learn and to express their growing understanding of STEM.

The STEM Institute provides a "family-style" feeling that lowers the student's anxiety about the school system. This characteristic of the program creates an atmosphere of trust and caring that encourages students to take academic chances in class. They participate in discussions, are willing to answer questions even when they are not sure, and support each other by clapping, cheering, and saying "good job" when one of their classmates provides an answer or works a problem on the board.

To prepare the teachers for their work in the STEM Institute, they attended a workshop, which provided training in cognitive psychology as well as guidelines and tools for designing units that will help their students advance to higher levels of thinking. One of the practices that the teachers found to be most helpful is to design units that span across all of the content areas, so that students can see the connections among the subjects that they are learning and how their learning relates to the real world beyond the walls of the school. They also came to agree on the following core idea, which they called a "STEM mind-set," for infusing into all of their classes:

> STEM is the manipulation of our natural world (science) through the engineering process, using mathematics as the tool for creation of the human made world (technology).

The teachers emphasize to the students that this idea is highly relevant to their lives because they will eventually join the community of adults who will apply STEM processes to help shape the human experience. The teachers have developed a number of creative units to communicate these important ideas and to challenge their students' preconceptions about the world around them. One of the most engaging is the unit that begins with the Frankenstein story, as described in the next section.

A Unit on Ethical Issues

One of the integrated units focuses on how people manipulate the natural world and the related ethical ramifications. This unit is implemented at the beginning of the school year for eighth graders and really kicks it off with a bang! For many students, it is the first time that they have considered human behavior and technological advancements from an ethical perspective. These considerations are a stepping-stone for the students as they begin to establish their personal beliefs. The cross-curricular design allows the students to explore their ethical positions from various angles. This allows the students to solidify and question their beliefs while they participate in the various activities.

To prepare for the beginning of the school year, the students are required to read the novel *Frankenstein* over the previous summer. Once school begins, there is very little organizational downtime and the students dive right into the integrated unit. This approach sets the academic and classroom management standards for the entire year.

The unit spans all subject areas, and each of the teachers incorporates ideas from the Frankenstein novel into their standards-based curriculum. In math class, the students design a Frankenstein "monster" using their own bodies as templates. They use tools to measure their own bodies, derive body proportions from their measurements, and then use the proportional relationships to create a scale drawing of their personal monsters, illustrating how it might be composed of various pieces. In science class, the students use the scale drawings from math class to design plans for assembling and activating their monsters.

In social studies class, the students' responses to the *Frankenstein* book provide a springboard for discussing three ethical issues that have been in the news: (1) euthanasia, (2) universal health care, (3) responses to bioterrorism. Their discussions of the ethical issues are enriched by work in their information and communications technology class, where they conduct research and build presentations to illustrate their findings. The students also design and conduct a schoolwide survey on current ethical issues. The survey results are analyzed and plotted using basic descriptive statistics toward the end of the unit in math class. And, of course, the language arts class focuses on the novel itself. All these activities combine to help students develop their ideas about complex ethical issues as they hone their skills in critical thinking, in addition to specific skills in mathematics, language arts, science, social studies, and information and communications technology.

Field Trip to a Hospital

One of the most important parts of this unit is the culminating field trip to a local hospital where students have an opportunity to discuss ethical issues and how they apply to real cases with doctors, including the head of the ethics committee. To prepare for the field trip, the teachers talk with their partners at the hospital and identify contemporary issues at the intersection of science and society that the students are expected to research and discuss in advance of the trip. The most recent list of questions includes:

- Should animals be used in pharmaceutical research?
- Should we inject women in their sixties with hormones that will allow them to have children?
- Should new life-forms be created to try to solve world problems such as hunger and pollution?
- Should we allow doctor-assisted suicide to hasten the death of terminally ill patients?
- Should stem cell research be continued?
- Should vast amounts of money be spent on space exploration when many people worldwide live in substandard conditions?
- Should we treat hereditary diseases by replacing defective genes?
- Should we use gene therapy techniques to improve an unborn child's appearance or intelligence potential?

Knowing that they will soon have an opportunity to talk about these issues with medical professionals helps to motivate the students to learn as much as they can before the field trip. These questions, combined with the novel's theme of right and wrong, moral and immoral, and what power people have over life and death make for some lively conversations in the classroom. The conversation at the hospital also provides assessment data to the teachers, as they witness how effectively the students are able to apply what they have been learning during a real-time conversation with professionals.

As students work across the curriculum, they begin to see the connections among the subjects and how each of them contributes to a broad understanding of important contemporary issues. This combination of content, activities, relevance, and performance assessment is one that the STEM Institute strives to achieve with every integrated unit. A table showing the sequence of the entire unit is shown in Figure 15.1.

Figure 15.1 Sequence of ethics unit based on Mary Shelley's *Frankenstein*.

Day of Unit	Math	Language Arts	Social Studies	Science	Biotech
1	Sets/Subsets and Timeline	Bioethics Vocabulary	Concept Mapping	Science Concept & Assessment	Bioethics PowerPoint
2	Make Venn Diagram	Bioethics Vocabulary	Concept Mapping	Engineering Concept & Assessment	Walk a Mile
3	Ratio/Rates	History– Mary Shelley	Current Event #1	Design Brief	Bioethics Beat on the Street
4	Proportions	Elements of a Story	Interpret Statistical Data	Design Prototype	Finalize Survey Questions
5	Similar Figures	Movie Poster	Interpret Statistical Data	Design Prototype	Conduct Survey
6	Scale Drawing of Monster	Bioethics Readings	Current Event #2	Movie Poster	Conduct Survey
7	Graph Math Relationships	Test–Frankenstein	Socratic Seminar	Create Monster from Scale Drawing	Analyze Survey Data
8	Field Trip	Field Trip	Field Trip	Field Trip	Field Trip
9	Scatter Plot and Biotech Data	Writing Prompt	Follow-up Activity	Complete Monster from Scale Drawing	Follow-up Activity

Putting the Pieces Together

Integrated units that stretch across the entire school curriculum take much planning, professional development, and district support. All of these components have to be clearly communicated so there is a shared understanding of expectations among the teachers and administrators. This level of planning can be difficult to achieve but is possible when the focus of the program is on creating the best possible educational experience for the students.

Professional development has also been essential to the success of the STEM Institutes. In addition to an initial workshop during which teachers from all of the institutes developed a common vocabulary and adopted common tools for creating integrated units, the teachers had opportunities to meet and plan during subsequent workshops. These additional professional development opportunities included updates on current educational research, time to work with industry partners to formulate new ideas, and a chance to bring new industry partners into the STEM Institute.

Working with industry partners also takes time, and two general methods evolved. In some cases a small group of teachers arranged to visit a partner's facility, where they could tour the facility and work with their partners to begin developing a unit. In the second method, teachers from all eight of the district's STEM Institutes came together at a school site to collaborate on ideas for new units with the help of industry partners. The second approach allowed the partners to see all the different STEM Institutes and network with a variety of teachers. The engagement by the industry partners generated by these collaborations has been tremendous and has helped to generate industry support for the entire school year.

At the beginning of each school year, all the STEM Institute teachers meet to work on their annual goals. The teacher teams create action plans and presentations about their institute and expectations for the school year. Action plan items include timelines, delineation of responsibilities of each task, marketing materials, classroom norms, classroom procedures, and other pieces based on our educational standards. These action plans are revisited each year to allow for districtwide goal inclusion, expansion, and modification of past practices. Each of the teachers expresses a commitment to professional development. Teachers who are not self-regulated lifelong learners struggle in this fluid environment, but the great majority of teachers thrive in our community of practice, based on values of family, trust, creativity, innovation, and desire to bring relevance to every lesson every day.

District-level support is essential to the success of these STEM Institutes. Due to the nature of curriculum integration, a large number of administrators are involved in fiscal and curricular decision making. These administrators hold decision-making power that can impact the future of these programs, teacher attitudes, and public opinion of the school. Indeed, the road is filled with potholes. To create a viable and effective support structure, one person is designated to be the communication gatekeeper for the STEM Institute. This lead teacher is responsible for all communication regarding field trips, media, needs from the district office, parental involvement, marketing, and internal communications at the school site. The system is designed so everyone knows who is responsible for each task.

Full Circle

The STEM Institutes are jewels in the Tampa Bay area, supported by district leaders and collaboration among a core team in science, career and technical education, and mathematics. Participation by language arts and social studies teachers in support of the STEM platform has greatly enriched the programs, helping students increase their skills in communication and civic engagement. Since the STEM Institutes were started four years ago, virtually all of the teachers have found the work to be tremendously exciting. In fact, one teacher retired and petitioned the superintendent to allow her to return to work as a volunteer so she could continue to work in this system.

The STEM Institute design is deeply rooted in the surrounding community. The parents have appreciated how excited their students are to go to school, even though they are expected to work hard to succeed in rigorous courses. And community partners have come to understand how an integrated curriculum model makes sense. This last observation has come as an epiphany to many of us. We have realized that we do not live in a well-structured world. We constantly face challenges in our daily lives, and we also encounter opportunities. These challenges and opportunities do not come neatly wrapped in packages labeled "science," "math," or "language arts." By learning in an integrated way, our students will be better prepared to solve the challenges and take advantage of the opportunities, using whatever knowledge and skills are appropriate to the task.

Reflection

- What do you think about the idea of creating STEM Institutes in your school or district? Is it desirable? Is it feasible? If so, how might you go about it?

- The integrated unit described in this chapter does not require that it be taught within a specially organized school, except that teachers do need to have the same students in common. If this is possible in your school, how might you go about developing and implementing an integrated unit that stretches all the way across the curriculum?

- Keep in mind that although it is best for a team of teachers to work together, individual teachers can also implement integrated lessons on their own. Are there some specific ideas in this chapter that you'd like to try?

REFERENCES

National Research Council. 2012. *A Framework for K–12 Science Education: Practices, Crosscutting Concepts, and Core Ideas.* Committee on a Conceptual Framework for New K–12 Science Education Standards. Board on Science Education, Division of Behavioral and Social Sciences and Education. Washington, DC: The National Academies Press. Available online at: www.nap.edu/catalog.php?record_id=13165.

Shelley, M. 1818. *Frankenstein, Or The Modern Prometheus.* London: Lackington, Hughes, Harding, Mavor, and Jones.

STEM LESSON ESSENTIALS • Integrating Science, Technology, Engineering, and Mathematics

CHAPTER 16

From Ripple to River
A Large Urban School District's Journey Moving STEM into the Main STREAMS

Some STEM for ALL and ALL STEM for Some

In support of the District STEM initiative, a comprehensive three-year framework is currently being developed with input from industry partners. The framework will ensure that all Orange County Public School students have experiences with problem-based learning that reinforces the collaborative nature of the 21st century workplace in elementary, middle, and early high school. For those students who demonstrate exceptional abilities in the areas of science, technology, engineering, and math, rigorous experiences will be available to extend the learning.

—Draft of a proposal to move STEM into the Main STREAMS,
prepared for the Executive Cabinet, Orange County (Florida) Public Schools

The following chapter was written by Mariel Milano, a STEM Resource Teacher in the Orange County (Florida) Public Schools.

BEFORE READING THIS CHAPTER, think about what it would take for your school district to undertake a major change in educational policy.

Disturbing the Still Water

A large school district is a lot like a pond of water. Change causes a small ripple on the surface, its effects far reaching and often unanticipated. Too many ripples or initiatives can make the surface of the water appear turbulent and unclear, making it impossible to peer through the once calm surface. This is the story of a large urban school district's journey from ripple. . . to brook . . . to stream . . . to roaring river of change.

Our Pond[1]

Orange County Public Schools (OCPS) is the tenth largest school district in the nation and the fourth largest in Florida. With over 12,000 teachers, 860 administrators, and nearly 180,000 students, bringing an initiative of any type to scale is a challenge.

Students in OCPS come from 212 countries and speak 162 different languages. Thirty-three percent of OCPS students are Hispanic, and 54 percent of all students receive free or reduced cost meals during the school day.

Divided into five learning communities, each with a distinct footprint but united under the district's superintendent, the schools are guided by the curriculum and pedagogical personnel at the Educational Leadership Center, which is home to the Division of Teaching and Learning and which includes the Curriculum and Instruction section. This central organization, in collaboration with teachers from throughout the district, has made it possible to develop and deploy STREAMS.

Ripples in the Pond

When the STEM initiative began, there were many ripples already in the pond. Groups of educators at various schools in the district were beginning the journey of STEM integration with replicable and scalable practices ready to emerge. We started with these groups to weave a more coherent and cohesive STEM initiative from the existing fibers of change. Several key questions guided this process:

- Why is there a need for change?
- What have other districts and states done with STEM integration?
- What STEM best practices already exist within our district?

---

[1] Data in this section are taken from Orange County Public Schools (OCPS) Pocket Facts 2010–2011.

Curriculum Services took several steps early on to ascertain the depth and breadth of existing STEM practices within the district: learning about and visiting STEM magnet schools, career academies, programs, clubs, and competitions and learning about our district's information technology strategic plan. As we expected, a lot of STEM activities were already going on. Our district was already rich in exciting STEM programs, including magnet programs in engineering, aeronautics, medicine, science, aviation, digital media and gaming, and global technology. We are one of Florida's leading providers of comprehensive secondary and postsecondary career and technical education programs, with courses offered at four tech centers on five campuses, nineteen high schools, thirty-four middle schools, various community and business sites, and our own Virtual Center.

It seemed as though true integration existed in some places. Nevertheless, all told, the existing STEM programs in the district reached only a small percentage of our students. Perhaps more troubling was that some students had no access at all to the *T* and *E* in *STEM*. The biggest surprise was that even at locations where excellent programs were being implemented, the number one question asked by teachers was, "What is STEM integration?"

As we began to think about how best to answer that question, it occurred to us that STEM didn't just have to be confined to science and math. To empower all students with access to STEM integration, we would have to attack the most sacred foundation in a public school system—the core curriculum. We began to ask ourselves, given current resources and time constraints, what would STEM integration look like in reading, mathematics, science, and social studies classrooms?

A Babbling Brook

OCPS is fortunate to have innovative leaders who recognized the value of bringing good initiatives to scale. With the ground for our STEM revolution already prepared by a strong commitment to the newly rewritten state standards, we began a nationwide search for successful districtwide STEM initiatives. We reviewed plans from Wisconsin, New York, Massachusetts, and Texas among others. Concurrently, the district took an active role in the Florida STEM Strategic Planning Committee to gain an even deeper understanding of the STEM programs in the surrounding districts.

Because purchasing curriculum to develop the initiative was not feasible, Curriculum Services reviewed existing curricular models (Engineering by Design, Project Lead the Way, Engineering Is Elementary, etc.) to identify integrative practices. The successful examples seemed to focus on engaging students in the engineering design process in which they would apply what they were learning in science and mathematics to address challenges at the local or global level.

We uncovered evidence from several district and curricular studies that indicated increased achievement by students involved in engineering design activities. This was significant, because the Florida Department of Education had classified OCPS as a high needs district due to the low performance of certain subpopulations, including English language learners (ELL) and special education students, on state science assessments given in grades 5, 8, and 11.

Moving STEM into the Main STREAMS

Streams are a lot like school systems—bound by the constraints of resources. Typically, each content area is its own stream, swept along by its own forces. Although it would be ideal from the STEM integration perspective to have a totally integrated curriculum, it is unrealistic, based not only on tradition but also on preservice education training and educator certification.

At times, the only way to perturb the system is to pretend it is not there and develop creative ways to integrate and then move back into each separate stream from a different angle, creating buy-in and incentives specific to each group. STEM integration was such a new concept in the core curriculum. We developed a draft executive summary of the concept for the Executive Cabinet, mapping the initiative to existing structures in the district and defining expectations for students and teachers, forming the bed of the stream. This chapter begins with a quote from the draft.

Top Down or Bottom Up?

Although teachers ultimately retain much autonomy over their classrooms, educational leaders play a crucial role in unifying expectations and allocating resources for those educators. Bearing that in mind, the leadership team decided to work both top-down and bottom-up. The STEM Resource Teacher launched a grassroots movement by meeting with existing STEM teacher leaders to plan how students can be expected to develop STEM skills as they advance through the grades, using as a guide the *Technology and Engineering Literacy Framework for the 2014 National Assessment of Educational Progress* (National Assessment Governing Board 2009).

Simultaneously, the leadership team recognized the need to build STEM capacity in the district curriculum staff to develop a common vision. Curriculum Services resource teachers, considered experts in their fields, are often the first line of communication at school sites. The STEM committee developed a STEM overview for the entire Curriculum Services department, so each resource teacher would feel confident sharing information about the budding initiative with school-based teacher leaders and administrators.

In the fall, the leadership team presented a STEM overview for Curriculum Services' district resource teachers describing the executive summary and building enthusiasm for the initiative. Curriculum Services then solicited interested district resource teachers to form a STEM committee and become "STEMbassadors." We took the time needed to get all of the key players on board because we were well aware that "disenfranchised people push a boulder uphill blindly frustrated and uncertain. Empowered people think of new ways to move the boulder uphill faster because they know why they are pushing" (author unknown).

We formed a STEM Committee comprised of innovative district resource teachers and administrators. Establishing this committee was a critical step to increase buy-in through teacher leadership. One of the key reasons widespread change is resisted is the fear factor. Fear that STEM would not truly "fit" in all content areas was a concern held by some. Who better than to address such a concern than colleagues from within their own content areas?

During each meeting of the STEM Committee, we refined our knowledge of design by modeling activities and discussing how this pedagogical approach would foster twenty-first-century learning skills. We identified meaningful misconceptions about STEM integration that we would later be able to address with our colleagues and developed the following measurable STEM outcomes.

- All students in pre-K–12 have at least a minimal level of engagement with STEM through problem-based learning in all content areas.
- Students in pre-K–12 have quarterly opportunities to create technology that meets the criteria and constraints of the client and is useful to the user. (Technology is dependent on the needs of people and cultures.)
- Students in grades 3–12 can define, explain, and implement the engineering design process within a variety of contexts.
- Students may use informational technology to communicate their findings and work collaboratively.
- Students in grade pre-K–12 will work collaboratively and communicate using grade-level identified technical and content-area vocabulary.
- By twelfth grade, students will be better able to define what engineering is and how engineers use mathematics, science, and technology.

Early in the process, the leadership team began to realize that even within Curriculum Services, the mental model of STEM integration was limited to well-worn ideas such as building bridges and egg drops. To expand and deepen the shared vision, each Curriculum Services STEMbassador developed a STEM integration station for use at the winter Curriculum Services staff meeting that would fully integrate engineering design into either a mathematics or science lesson. Some of the STEM activity stations included designing a cooler, a programming sequence for Dance Mania, a parking garage, an igloo, a snowflake, a suitcase, and a system for forecasting winter storms. After all staff members had a chance to dive in and experience STEM integration at one station, the whole group had the opportunity to identify "aha moments" and discuss similarities and trends between activities, creating an operational definition of STEM integration.

STEM LESSON ESSENTIALS • Integrating Science, Technology, Engineering, and Mathematics

Investigating the possibilities for STEM integration in a nonthreatening setting paid huge dividends, as the conversation began to spread into each content
area on how design-based learning could be incorporated into plans for summer writing teams. One looming trepidation: "How can the Curriculum Services be sure that this type of learning will prepare students for the workplace?"

Where Will the River Meet the Ocean?

The long-term goal of this effort is to create a sustainable educational model
that will enable OCPS to help today's students become twenty-first-century
thinkers who can compete in a competitive global marketplace and participate
in rigorous postsecondary educational opportunities. To figure out how to do
that, we had to address the essential question: "How can we prepare students
for a world that we do not yet know?"

Central Florida is home to robust STEM industries, most notably biotechnology and simulation, which are among the largest employers in the region.
Recognizing the need to align educational practices with growing workforce
demands, local industrial leaders formed the Central Florida STEM Education
Council (CFSTEM). As Curriculum Services grappled with how to meaning-
fully embed STEM and twenty-first-century skills into summer writing teams,
they turned to CFSTEM for assistance. Members of the STEM Committee were
invited to visit STEM workplaces such as Boeing, Harris Corporation, Northrop
Grumman, Disney, and Florida Hospital in cross-curricular teams to view
twenty-first-century skills being put to work in a wide variety of contexts. Upon
returning, each STEM Committee member shared the most impactful moment
of their visit with the whole department and then led a cross-curricular focus
group in identifying district-level curricular implications based on the specific job-shadowing experiences. Insights from these experiences included the
following:

- Teamwork is essential.
- Collaboration is more than sitting together.

- Students need to think critically, not just memorize formulas.
- It is more important to know how to find the answer than to know the answer.
- Students need to be able to apply what they have learned.
- We must build risk takers.
- We should promote our students' individual strengths.
- Knowledge of technical writing is important.
- We must encourage our students' imaginations and communications skills.

Defining the Banks of the Stream

Based on the findings from these visits to STEM rich industries and subsequent discussions, it became clear that twenty-first-century skills included more than just the four traditional STEM fields. The workers of tomorrow needed reading and writing skills; they needed to be able to communicate verbally and through art. They needed the broader context that was available through social studies. In short, it was time for STEM to become STREAMS (**S**cience, **T**echnology, **R**eading, **E**ngineering, **A**rts, **M**athematics, and **S**ocial Studies), and to take into account our special education students and our English language learners. Consequently, we expanded our circle and started strategic planning sessions to identify long- and short-term goals with our colleagues in early childhood education, fine arts, social studies, and English language arts. We met separately with resource teachers in these areas. By meeting with these groups within their comfortable silos, each group had an opportunity to focus on the goals and objectives of their content area, to be sure that what they considered to be important could be accomplished through integration. We developed long- and short-term goals for STREAMS in each area at all four grade-level bands: pre-K–2, 3–5, 6–8, and 9–12.

The strategic planning sessions resulted in a comprehensive three-year framework with input from industry partners that ensured that all OCPS students would have experiences with problem-based learning that would reinforce the collaborative nature of the twenty-first-century workplace in elementary, middle, and early high school. The three-year plan, which we have followed quite closely, is sketched in Figure 16.1.

Beginning in early childhood, students would have quarterly technology design opportunities in mathematics and science as part of the core curriculum. As part of the extended curriculum, embedded design opportunities would also exist in the special areas of art and music. These opportunities would scaffold through high school where STEM career academies, magnet programs, and competitions would provide extended learning opportunities for those who demonstrated exceptional abilities—thus, enacting the concept "Some STEM for ALL and ALL STEM for Some."

Figure 16.1 Strategic plan for moving STEM into the main STREAMS.

Strategic Plan for Moving STEM into the Main STREAMS	
Year 1	**Problem-Based Learning in Early Childhood and Elementary School**
	• Interdisciplinary quarterly science based design challenges • Interdisciplinary quarterly mathematics design challenges (pre-K–2) • Interdisciplinary quarterly model eliciting activities (3–5) • Biannual design units in art and music • Annual STEM fair
Year 2	**Problem-Based Learning in Middle School**
	• Interdisciplinary quarterly science-based design challenges • Interdisciplinary quarterly model eliciting activities • Biannual design units in art and wellness • Increased participation in STEM fair • OCPS "Design Squad"-themed environmental engineering competition • 8th grade job shadowing opportunities for students and teachers • Increase interest in STEM magnet program development
Year 3	**Problem-Based Learning in High School**
	• 9th grade introduction to design for all students through physical science • 9th grade job shadowing opportunities for students and teachers • Physics-First science course progression to increase access to STEM • Interdisciplinary quarterly design challenges in science disciplines • Interdisciplinary quarterly model eliciting activities in geometry and algebra

A Swiftly Moving River

Once a change takes hold, it moves swiftly, and the opportunity for convergence between two rushing streams to form a river becomes possible. The push for increased rigor in twenty-first-century skills had begun to sweep in waves throughout the district. As news of the pilot programs grew at the elementary level, school-based teacher leaders received introductory professional development on STEM integration. Curriculum Services personnel held STEM integration trainings for Reading Coaches, Mathematics Specialists, Curriculum Resource Teachers, and Elementary Science Lead Teachers in year one. School-based teacher leaders then shared the information they have received through a Train the Trainer Model.

Acknowledging that problem-based learning was key to accessing those skills, Curriculum Services leaders also convened the first cross-curricular writing teams. These teams created sample cross-curricular lessons, which laid the foundation for the use of problem-based learning in writing teams.

Development of new cross-curricular lessons for the elementary level continued with the help of Engineering Teachers-in-Residence as well as teacher leaders who had participated in district STEM professional development were selected for participation. They joined elementary writing teams focused on mathematics, science, art, and reading, serving as the STEM experts and working collaboratively with others to revise or develop STEM design challenges. The Curriculum Services team worked with the teams to develop lesson planning maps, which guided STEM writing team members in weaving together standards from each content area into a single engineering-influenced cohesive story.

Each map begins by identifying the primary focus subject. The planning map outlines critical steps in development of an OCPS STREAMS lesson. After the design challenge is tested in the classroom and mapped, it is transferred to the district's Completed STEM Lesson Plan template, linking it back to twenty-first-century thinking skills and organized according to the 5E model (Engage, Explore, Explain, Elaborate, Evaluate) with its correlation to the engineering design process. These templates are shown in Figures 16.2, 16.3, and 16.4.

STEM LESSON ESSENTIALS • Integrating Science, Technology, Engineering, and Mathematics

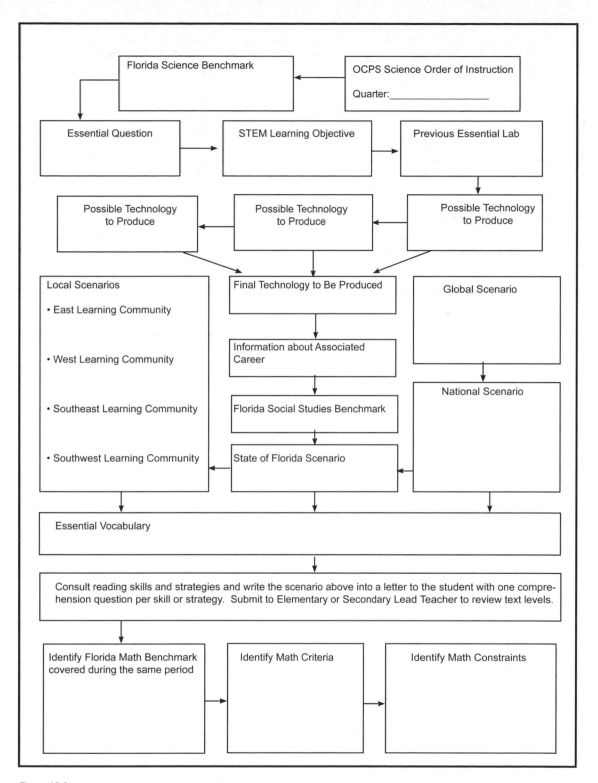

Figure 16.2 STEM lesson planning map: template part 1.

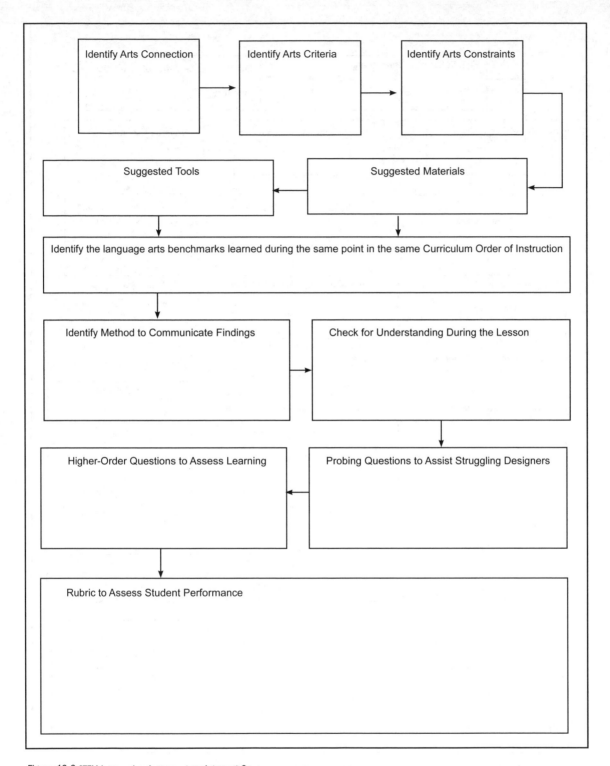

Figure 16.3 STEM lesson planning map: template part 2.

STEM LESSON ESSENTIALS • Integrating Science, Technology, Engineering, and Mathematics

STEM Curriculum, Instruction, Assessment Lesson Plan	
Lesson Objectives	Standard(s)/Benchmarks Addressed
Essential Question(s)	New Vocabulary
Higher-Order Question(s)	
Twenty-First-Century Skills to Increase Rigor (check) O Teamwork and collaboration O Initiative and leadership O Curiosity and imagination O Innovation and creativity O Critical thinking and problem solving O Flexibility and adaptability O Effective oral and written communication O Accessing and analyzing information	Instructional Strategies Accommodations
Background information for teachers Lesson activity and experiences	
The ABCs of Inquiry = Activity Before Concept, Concept Before Vocabulary, and then Read	
Lesson Cycle	
Engage/Ask Ideas to check for understanding:	
Explore/Imagine Ideas to check for understanding:	
Explain/Design Ideas to check for understanding:	
Elaborate/Create Ideas to check for understanding:	
Evaluate/Redesign Ideas to check for understanding:	
Evidence of Learning (What does it look like? What does it sound like? What do I do next?)	
Materials/Resources Needed	

Figure 16.4 Completed STEM lesson plan template.

How many times have students asked, "Why are we learning this?" or "What will I ever do with this?" STEM design challenges address the "So what?" factor in the classroom. All real-world scenarios relating to a specific engineering design challenge are shared with students at the inception of a unit of study as the catalyst for inquiring further about the concept. At the conclusion of the unit, the students apply what they've learned and use the engineering design process to propose a solution as a performance assessment.

Is the Stream Still Flowing?

Maintaining the flow of problem-based design and inquiry throughout the district is essential to maintain momentum. Currently, STEM workshops and virtual Web courses that focus on best practices related to engineering design are being conducted at various sites. Although it appears that a paradigm shift is occurring, we are keeping in mind that we need to "inspect what we expect."

In a high accountability system, we cannot expect teachers to devote valuable time to content that is not assessed. Although many may hope to shift the focus off high-stakes testing as a driving force behind curriculum, it is a motivating factor for many teachers. To this end, Curriculum Services piloted STEM-based performance tasks in the district fifth-grade science benchmark exams. These questions, which were modeled after Massachusetts released test items, asked students to apply their understanding of science to evaluate real-world design solutions. These questions have added significant rigor, in keeping with Florida's new state standards and assessments. They have also encouraged teachers to incorporate more STEM lessons and demonstrated to students how what they are learning in school applies to the real world.

Our Curriculum Services team is developing a *STEM Continuum of Implementation* guide that articulates what STEM "looks like" if implemented: (1) in name only; (2) intentionally structured; or (3) culturally embedded. District- and school-based administrators will be able to utilize the continuum in classroom walk-through visits and professional learning communities. To provide positive reinforcement, district resource teachers will visit schools on a day of their choos-

STEM LESSON ESSENTIALS • Integrating Science, Technology, Engineering, and Mathematics

ing, and based on their observations, they will choose a STEM-tastic School of the Month. STEM-tastic schools will be recognized on the district STEM portal along with a brief summary of their STEM programs.

Suggestions for Starting a STEM Initiative in Your School District

- Start small. Ask teachers to implement a limited but quantifiable amount of STEM lessons each year.
- Provide problem-based learning training for all classroom teachers, with more extensive training for teacher leaders.
- Involve administrators at every level of implementation. Support from district and school administration will foster buy-in and validate the shift in focus.
- Capitalize on the use of professional learning communities as vehicles for STEM integration.
- Coordinate and consolidate initiatives. (We consolidated the STEM initiative with the more established initiative for twenty-first-century thinking skills.)
- Begin with the end in mind. Begin using cohorts of elementary students. This will make data easier to track as well as allow time for resources to increase gradually.
- Anticipate and disarm potential conflicts in implementation before they arise.

From Many Streams to a Mighty River . . . Where Will It Take Us?

Like a swiftly flowing river, our efforts to move STEM into the core curriculum through all subjects at all levels continues to gain momentum and seek out new channels. On the near horizon are plans to expand professional development and increase the availability of STEM resources in middle school and high schools. We will focus the initiative on college and career readiness through activities such as job shadowing for teachers and students. The goal of these opportunities will be to increase awareness of how STEM knowledge and skills are used in the real world and to set learning expectations so that classroom activities can begin to mirror the level of rigor required in the workplace.

Plans are also taking shape with industry and informal science education partners to develop districtwide grade-level field trips that highlight STEM integration experiences not possible in the classroom. For example, we are partnering with Headquarter Honda, which owns the highest LEED (Leadership in Energy and Environmental Design) certified building in the state of Florida, which features a rooftop garden, solar panels, and rainwater reclamation. An initial project will engage OCPS students in Advanced Placement Environmental Science, who will tour the facility and then design their own model building that maximizes energy efficiency and minimizes its carbon footprint.

Since the inception of the STEM initiative in OCPS, a number of clear and coherent STREAMS have converged into a single powerful river that is cutting deeply into the educational landscape of central Florida. As the initiative continues, it will allow us to meet the increasingly rigorous demands of the twenty-first century so that we can better prepare our students for the global marketplace.

Reflection

- What are your thoughts about the reforms enacted in the Orange County Public Schools? What do you think about the guiding principle: Some STEM for ALL and ALL STEM for Some?

- In your opinion, are certain elements of the plan most important and feasible to replicate elsewhere? Or is the plan as a whole more important for improving STEM education?

- How would such a plan function in your school district? How might it be implemented?

REFERENCES

National Assessment Governing Board. 2010. *Technology and Engineering Literacy Framework for the 2014 National Assessment of Educational Progress*. Available at: www.nagb.org/publications/frameworks/prepub_naep_tel_framework_2014.pdf.

Wagner, T. 2008, 2010. *The Global Achievement Gap: Why Even Our Best Schools Don't Teach the New Survival Skills Our Children Need—And What We Can Do About It*. New York: Basic Books.

STEM LESSON ESSENTIALS • Integrating Science, Technology, Engineering, and Mathematics

CHAPTER 17

Resources for Creating STEM Curricula

Good leaders, like good designers or good curators, recognize the rare skill of combining things together well. . . . There's a time to reinvent and a time to reuse, and the best minds know that both approaches have their place.

—"Stop Trying to Reinvent the Wheel," Scott Berkun (2010)

There are many exciting projects and lesson plans available on the Web for teaching and learning STEM at all grade levels. In many cases, you may find that the instructional materials you need have already been developed, and they only need to be adapted in small ways to meet the needs of your students. In other cases, you may need to do more development, but require some initial ideas to get started. This chapter suggests a few resources to help you on your way. Nearly all of these resources are available for free or low cost.

Obviously there are great organizations such as the National Science Teachers Association (www.nsta.org), and the National Council of Teachers of

Mathematics (www.nctm.org) are good beginning sites for STEM resources. Other great websites include:

- **American Association for the Advancement of Science (AAAS), Science NetLinks: http://sciencenetlinks.com**
  You will find K–12 lesson plans and information for planning new activities for Earth Day, National Chemistry Week, National Engineers Week.

- **ASCD Express: Preparing Students for a STEM-Filled World: www.ascd.org/ascd-express/vol6/624-toc.aspx**
  This issue of ASCD's Express features promising initiatives that seek to bridge the STEM content gap for both students and educators. The National Science Teachers Association (NSTA) offers advice and resources to help teachers engage their students in STEM subjects.

- **Discovery Education: www.discoveryeducation.com/teachers**
  Digital science and technology resources offer a rich, engaging, educational experience. Content is aligned with national standards and they have lesson plans that include objectives, materials, procedures, readings, and resources as well as assessment ideas. Don't miss the puzzlemaker application at www.discoveryeducation.com/free-puzzlemaker.

- **Edutopia: http://www.edutopia.org/groups**
  This site will get you started with project-based units and assessment ideas as well as other great tools and strategies for effective STEM teaching.

- **Federal Resources for Educational Excellence: http://free.ed.gov**
  This site provides projects related to oceanography, evolution, botany, and bioethics. They have ideas for building solar cars, lesson plans, games, homework assignments, and 150 math websites that are linked onto their site.

- **High-Quality STEM Education for English Learners: Current Challenges and Effective Practices: www.ncela.gwu.edu/meetings/stem forum/#panel**

The U.S. Department of Education's Office for English Language Acquisition hosted a forum on educating English learners in STEM fields. Visit the website to read materials from the conference and access to the speakers' presentations.

- **Intel Education's Design and Discovery Curriculum: http://educate.intel.com/en/designdiscovery**

  This site provides you with their design and discovery curriculum, which is free, with interdisciplinary and project-based learning projects already done for you. This curriculum is for students ages 11–15, though it can be adapted for lower grades. Intel STEM unit plans can be found at www.intel.com/about/corporate responsibility/education/k12/STEM Units.htm.

- **Khan Academy: www.khanacademy.org**

  The celebrated Khan Academy offers more than 2,700 instructional videos covering math, science, finance, and history. They are short instructional videos that may be appropriate to help build your own content knowledge.

- **The Museum of Science, Boston, Technology and Engineering Curriculum (TEC) Review: www.mos.org/tec**

  This site provides detailed reviews by experienced teachers of hundreds of instructional materials on technology and engineering, including many that are integrated with science and mathematics. A convenient search engine makes it possible to quickly search the database for materials by grade level, topic, or state standard alignments.

- **National Science Digital Library's K–6 Science refreshers: http://nsdl.org/refreshers/science**

  This site provides teachers with a quick review of science concepts. From weather to electricity to simple machines to paleoclimates, there are tons of minilessons and also modules, quizzes, and links to additional resources.

- **National STEM Video Game Challenge: http://stemchallenge.org**

  This site will help your students participate in a competition that will really motivate them. The website helps students learn about game design and resources and then they can enter the national competition.

- **PBS Teachers STEM Education Resource Center: www.pbs.org/teachers/stem**

  With more than four thousand STEM resources available in its database, this website has a vast array of lesson plans, videos, and interactive resources to help you infuse both fun and rigor into your STEM lessons.

- **NASA's Planet Quest Exoplanet Exploration: http://planetquest.jpl.nasa.gov**

  Interested in space exploration? Learn from the experts about space exploration. This website is sponsored by NASA's Jet Propulsion Laboratory (JPL) and the California Institutes of Technology. The comprehensive, interactive Planet Quest website features spectacular images captured by NASA's Hubble Space Telescope; the Ask an Astronomer podcast; videos; classroom experiments; and JPL blog, which will take you inside a space mission. They also have a Digital Learning Network at www.nasa.gov/offices/education/programs/national/dln.

- **National Academy Press website: www.NAP.edu**

  This site includes many very useful reports from the National Research Council, most available for free download. For example, several reports that are especially relevant to STEM education include: *A Framework for K–12 Science Education: Practices, Crosscutting Concepts, and Core Ideas* (2012); *Taking Science to School: Learning and Teaching Science in Grades K–8* (2007); *Learning Science in Informal Settings: People, Places, and Pursuits* (2009); *Technologically Speaking: Why All Americans Need to Learn More About Technology* (2002); and *How People Learn: Brain, Mind, Experience, and School* (1999).

- **National Commission on Teaching and America's Future (NCTAF): http://jctaf.org/NCTAFReportNSFKnowledgeSynthesis.htm**

  The NCTAF released a report in collaboration with National Science Foundation (NSF) and WestEd entitled *STEM Teachers in Professional*

STEM LESSON ESSENTIALS • Integrating Science, Technology, Engineering, and Mathematics

Learning Communities: From Good Teacher to Great Teaching. This report provides a two-year analysis of the research around what happens when STEM teachers work together in professional learning communities to improve teaching and increase student achievement.

- **Science, Technology, Engineering, and Mathematics (STEM) Education Coalition: www.stemedcoalition.org/**

  This organization works to support STEM programs for teachers and students at the U.S. Department of Education, the National Science Foundation, and other agencies that offer STEM-related programs. It represents all sectors of the technological workforce and is dedicated to ensuring quality STEM education at all levels. The website contains reference resources and reports on national and state STEM initiatives.

- **Science, Technology, Engineering, and Mathematics (STEM) Education Institute at the University of Massachusetts Amherst: http://umassk12.net/stem/**

  The Institute's work is to improve STEM education in K–12 and higher education. The website contains information on projects, educational resources, and teacher workshops.

- **Successful K–12 STEM Education: Identifying Effective Approaches in STEM, a study by the National Research Council: www.nap.edu**

  This report, available for a small fee from the National Academies Press website, outlines the indicators for a STEM-focused school, curriculum, and practices. It provides information to help make strategic decisions about improving STEM education within a system.

- **TEACH Engineering.org: http://www.teachengineering.org**

  This searchable, Web-based digital library collection is populated with standards-based engineering curricula including many with connections with mathematics and science disciplines. These resources for K–12 were developed by a collaborative of faculty from five universities and the American Society for Engineering Education, with funding from the NSF National Science Digital Library. The collection continues to grow and evolve over time with new additions from other universities and input from teachers who use the curricula in their classrooms.

- **Thornberg Center for Space Exploration: www.tcse-k12.org**
  The mission of the Thornberg Center for Space Exploration is to inspire students and improve STEM education through the design and implementation of an international program on Space Exploration. A paper by David Thornberg posted on its website at http://www.tcse-k12.org/pages/stem.pdf makes a strong case for integration of the STEM disciplines.

REFERENCE

Berkun S. 2010. "Stop Trying to Reinvent the Wheel." *Bloomberg Business Week* June 2. Available at: www.businessweek.com/innovate/content/jun2010/id2010062_565850.htm.

STEM LESSON ESSENTIALS • Integrating Science, Technology, Engineering, and Mathematics